Massacre at Fort William Henry

Massacre at
Fort William Henry

David R. Starbuck

UNIVERSITY PRESS OF NEW ENGLAND

HANOVER AND LONDON

UNIVERSITY PRESS OF NEW ENGLAND, HANOVER, NH 03755

PRINTED IN THE UNITED STATES OF AMERICA

5   4   3   2   1

LIBRARY OF CONGRESS CATALOGING-IN-PUBLICATION DATA

Starbuck, David R.
    Massacre at Fort William Henry / David R. Starbuck.
        p.   cm.
    Includes bibliographical references (p.   ) and index.
    ISBN 1–58465–166–0 (pbk. : alk. paper)
        1. Fort William Henry (N.Y.) — Capture, 1757. 2. Massacres — New York
(State) — Fort William Henry — History — 18th century. 3. Fort William
Henry (N.Y.) — Antiquities. 4. Fort William Henry (N.Y.) — Biography.
5. Lake George Region (N.Y.) — Antiquities. 6. Indians of North
America — New York (State) — Lake George Region — History — 18th century.
    I. Title.
E199 .S786 2002
973.2'6—dc21   2001004770

Frontispiece: Detail of "A Plan of Fort William Henry" (fig. 2.1).
Courtesy of J. Robert Maguire.

Contents

Preface

I first visited Fort William Henry when I was in the fourth grade, and I have returned many times since then, always impressed by the sad and heroic events that transpired at this small frontier fort at the south end of Lake George. Now that my colleagues and I have completed four years of archeological excavations at this famous site, it is finally time to reveal what archeology has painstakingly gleaned from the charred ruins of the log fort. When I was a youngster walking through the reconstructed fort, I certainly did not intend to write a book about what was once the foremost outpost of British expansion into the interior of America. However, so much new research was conducted in the 1990s, all of it sponsored by Adirondack Community College, that it is now possible to tell the story in a way that could not have been done by scholars of previous generations.

Because the history of Fort William Henry has already been the subject of several other books, I have tried not to repeat every known historical detail. After all, this is a study of what has survived to the present day: the ruins, the artifacts, the human bones, and more. It is also a historiography of how attitudes toward the fort and the "massacre" have changed from the 1750s up to the present, especially given the tremendous influence of James Fenimore Cooper's great novel, *The Last of the Mohicans.* Myths clearly have a tendency to replace fact, and while the early-twentieth-century image that I selected for the cover of this book may convey the "feel" of the massacre, it is woefully inaccurate in that it depicts Conestoga wagons on the shores of Lake George. This is an old and much-distorted story, but archaeology is helping to make it a new story again.

I wish to thank Phyllis Deutsch, my editor at the University Press of New England, for constant encouragement as this volume proceeded over the past two years; and I would like to thank friends and administrators at Adirondack Community College for their unfailing support of the fieldwork behind this research. I also wish to thank the directors and staff of the Fort William Henry Corporation for granting us permission to excavate at the fort from 1997 until the present. Thanks are especially due to Robert Flacke Sr., Robert Flacke Jr., Kathy Muncil, Dawn Littrell, Mary Ann Urch, and Gerald Bradfield. Gerry, the curator of Fort William Henry since late 1997, has been invaluable in answering our questions, allowing us to use his office, and encouraging us to keep making new discoveries.

Carleton Dunn, who excavated at the fort in the 1950s, has been an invaluable source of information about past work at the fort. Equally helpful has been Ed O'Dell, a professional photographer who not only printed nearly all of the images in this book but also did the darkroom work for Stanley Gifford when he directed excavations at the fort in the 1950s. This continuity with the past has made our own work much more rewarding.

Most of all, I am indebted to the archeological staff and the many students and volunteers who have dug with me at Fort William Henry, including our laboratory supervisor, Merle Parsons; our field supervisors, Matthew Rozell, Brad Jarvis, Andy Farry, John Farrell, John Kosek, and Susan Winchell-Sweeney; and our surveyors, Gordon and Barbara De Angelo. They were joined by nearly two hundred excavators and laboratory workers. It is impossible to list everyone who has worked with us, but those who have participated for two or more seasons include Ashley Andrews, Judith Balyeat, Bruce Batten, Joshua Blackler, Herman Brown, Betsey Brownell, Kathleen Burg, James Campbell, Cathleen Catalfamo, Albert Clarke, Meghan Cormie, Kate Cosseboom, Adam Czapliaski, Marie Ellsworth, Jeremy Farrell, Linda Fuerderer, Stephen Fuller, Heather Gilman, Emily Griffith, Elizabeth Hall, Brett Harper, Fred Harris, Philip Haubner, Bruce Hedin, William Herrlich, Laurens Jansen, Maureen Kennedy, William Ketchum, Leah Larcenaire, Naton Leslie, Abby Locke, George Martin, Ray Matteau, Roy Mattson, Abigail McGuirk, Bob Miettunen, Gini Miettunen, Melanie Morehouse, Jillian Mulder, William Murphy, Scott Padeni, Anjali Paranjpe, Fred Patton, Tori Porter, Dodi Robinson, Nichole Rogers, Victor Rolando, Jene Romeo, Avtar Shepherd-Singh, Roland Smith, Gerd Sommer, Dorothy Stanton, Richard Stickel, June Talley, Don Thompson, Mark Van Valkenburg, Sarah Waite, Renee Walker, Buck Welch, Rusty Welch, Linda White, Diane Wood, and Claudia Young-Palmer. Many of our diggers, especially John Farrell, contributed to Appendix 1 by recording some of the more pithy sayings made by visitors to the fort.

I also wish to single out and thank Merle Parsons, who tabulated many of the artifacts from our excavations (summarized in tables in this book) and Jene Romeo (Hunter College, CUNY), who most graciously shared with me some of the results of her analyses of the foodways at Fort William Henry. Robert Funk and Louise Basa examined many of the prehistoric artifacts from our excavation, and I am grateful for their identifications. Steve Comer, a member of the Stockbridge-Munsee Band of the Mohicans, was an excellent source of information about the Mohicans of the historical period. Also, I am grateful for the help I received from Grace MacDonald, historian for the Town of Lake George, and Margaret Edwards, historian for the Village of Lake George. Both Grace and Margaret were generous with historical sources and provided some of the illustrations that are included here.

Finally, I wish to thank Naton Leslie, professor of English at Siena College, for hours spent in discussion, considering the role of James Fenimore Cooper and his contributions to American literature. I am indebted to Nate for helping me to realize that this book had to touch upon many issues and not be limited to a description of some archeological finds.

I hope that our efforts have helped to bring new and positive attention to the important events that transpired at Fort William Henry between 1755 and 1757, and we are grateful to have had the opportunity to contribute to one of colonial America's most enduring stories.

January 2001   D.R.S.

Chronology of Fort William Henry and the Lake George Area

1646   Father Isaac Jogues claims "Lac du St. Sacrement" for France.

1755   (Sept. 8) The Battle of Lake George pits the British under General William Johnson against the French under Baron Dieskau; Colonel Ephraim Williams and King Hendrick are killed, but the British win. During the battle, a group of French and Indians are surprised and killed, and their bodies are thrown into "Bloody Pond."

   (Sept.) The French begin construction of Fort Carillon (Ticonderoga) on Lake Champlain. Captain William Eyre begins construction of Fort William Henry.

1757   (March 19) The French, led by François-Pierre de Rigaud de Vaudreuil, attack Fort William Henry.

   (July 23) The French, led by Joseph Marin de la Malgue, attack Fort Edward.

   (July 26) The French destroy the New Jersey Regiment ("Jersey Blues") near Sabbath Day Point on Lake George.

   (August 3–9) The French, led by the Marquis de Montcalm, conduct the siege of Fort William Henry.

   (August 9) The British surrender Fort William Henry, and Indians kill the wounded inside the fort.

   (August 10) The retreating British, with a French escort, are attacked by Indians on the military road to Fort Edward; this becomes known as the "massacre."

   (August 11–12) Fort William Henry is burned to the ground, and the French depart for Fort Carillon.

1758   (March 11) The Battle on Snowshoes, between Rogers' Rangers and the French, is fought near Rogers Rock.

   (June–July) General James Abercromby's army occupies the ruins of Fort William Henry.

   (July 8) Abercromby's army attacks the French at Fort Carillon and withdraws with massive losses.

(August 8) The French and Rogers' Rangers fight the "Battle of Fort Anne."

1759   (July) General Jeffrey Amherst's army camps atop the ruins of Fort William Henry and begins construction of Fort George. Amherst's army captures Fort Carillon and renames it "Ticonderoga."

(Sept. 13) General James Wolfe's army attacks Quebec, the capital of New France, and the city surrenders to the British a few days later; both Wolfe and Montcalm are killed.

(Oct. 6) Rogers' Rangers raid the Abenaki village of Saint Francis (Odanak).

1760   (Sept. 8) Montreal falls to the British.

1763   The Treaty of Paris ends the French and Indian War and with it many of France's claims to North America.

1783   (August) General George Washington visits the site of Fort William Henry.

1826   James Fenimore Cooper pens *The Last of the Mohicans*.

1854   Construction of the first Fort William Henry Hotel. Williams College erects a monument to the memory of Ephraim Williams at the side of Route 9.

1870   The Fort William Henry Hotel is destroyed by fire and in the following year is replaced by a structure that will accommodate nine hundred persons.

1872   The site of Fort William Henry is sold to the Lake Champlain Transportation Company, later affiliated with the Delaware & Hudson Railroad Company.

1903   The Lake George Battle Monument is erected in the Battlefield Park by the Society of Colonial Wars.

1908   The Fort William Henry Hotel burns.

1911   The second (technically the third) Fort William Henry Hotel opens, under the ownership of the Delaware & Hudson Railroad Company.

1936   *The Last of the Mohicans* opens at movie theaters, starring Randolph Scott.

1952   The Fort William Henry Corporation is formed, and archeological excavations begin at the site of Fort William Henry.

1955   The reconstruction of Fort William Henry is completed.

1966   A fire inside the reconstructed West Barracks of Fort William
       Henry destroys many of the artifacts recovered in the 1950s.

1969   The second (technically the third) Fort William Henry Hotel is
       removed and subsequently replaced by the Fort William Henry
       Motor Inn.

1992   *The Last of the Mohicans* opens at movie theaters, starring Daniel
       Day-Lewis.

1997   Archeological excavations begin at Fort William Henry under
       the sponsorship of Adirondack Community College.

Massacre at Fort William Henry

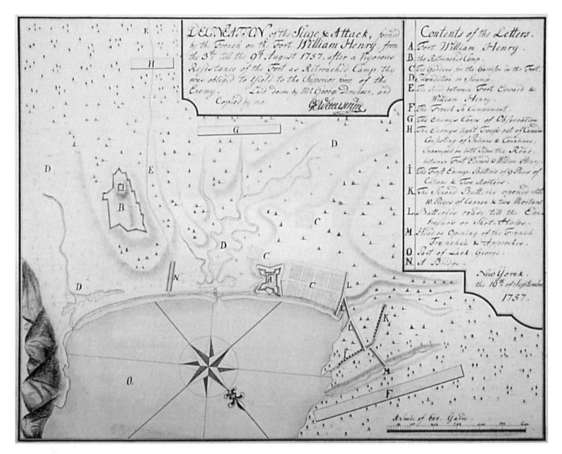

FIG. 1.1. "DELINEATION of the Siege & Attack, formed by the French on the Fort William Henry, from the 3[the] till the 9th August 1757, after a Vigorous Resistance of the Fort as Retrenched Camp thy was obliged to Yield to the Superior force of the Enemy, Laid down by Mr George Demelaer, and Copied by me GC Wetterstrom."

The legend lists: "A. Fort William Henry. B. the Retrenched Camp. C. The Gardens for the Garrison in the Fort. D. Inondation or Swamp. E. The Road between Fort Edward & William Henry. F. The French In Campement. G. The Enemys Corps of Observation. H. The Enemys light Troups out of Canada Consisting of Indians & Canadians, Incamped on both Sides the Road, between Fort Edward & William Henry. i. The First Enemys Batterie of 9 Pieces of Canons & Two Mortars. K. The Second Batterie opened with 10. Pieces of Cannon & two Mortars. L. Batteries ready till the Embrasurs or Shot. Holes. M. Head or Opening of the French Trenchee & Approches. O. Part of Lack. George. N. A Bridge. New Yorek. the 19th of Septembr. 1757." Courtesy of J. Robert Maguire.

Chapter 1

The History of the Fort

Background

LAKE GEORGE OFFERS one of the most beautiful vistas in America, a long finger of blue water resting against the eastern side of the Adirondack Mountains in New York State. Over the past ten thousand years it has evolved from the home of Native Americans to the staging area for determined British armies in the eighteenth century to one of the finest vacation destinations in the United States. This region is now typified by water sports, fine restaurants, and easy access to Albany and New York City via the Adirondack Northway. But this idyllic setting cannot erase from memory the tragedy that visited the southern shore of Lake George in August of 1757. The siege and massacre that crushed the garrison of a small log fort, Fort William Henry, was the most horrific event of the decades-long conflict between the French and British for mastery of the American colonies.

Our knowledge of Fort William Henry is provided by engineers' drawings (see fig. 1.1), contemporary soldiers' and officers' diaries, newspaper accounts, subsequent retellings by nineteenth-century historians, and more sophisticated analysis by a handful of writers in the twentieth century. Although Fort William Henry was one of many frontier forts, its story is more colorful and more somber than most because of the overpowering assault upon its walls. The fort's spirited defenders bravely held out against overwhelming odds, only to have part of the garrison killed and mutilated after they finally surrendered to the French seven days later. These events were to dramatically affect the attitudes of British settlers toward the French and their Indian allies for generations to come. While the specifics of this engagement may not be well known to most Americans or Canadians today, the brutal actions of the French and Indians produced a powerful response of hatred and fear that still lingers within the region. The massacre at Fort William Henry was, for its time, every bit as dramatic and inspirational as was the fall of the

Alamo nearly a century later or the destruction of Pearl Harbor almost two centuries later.

While the downfall of Fort William Henry is more significant and memorable than many other eighteenth-century events, it still must be reanalyzed by each generation according to changing cultural perspectives. And although primary sources have been repeatedly examined by scholars, archeology now permits us to examine the site itself as though it were a newly discovered document just waiting to tell us what went terribly wrong inside a colonial fort. In this book, historical archeology uses the ruins and artifacts of the past, together with the written record, to draw new insights from America's best-known colonial tragedy. That is what makes *Massacre at Fort William Henry* an original work, not simply the next scholarly effort to retell a 250-year-old story.

Part of what makes this a great drama is that none of the controversies pertaining to the fort has ever been resolved, and scholarly interpretations diverge on every aspect of what happened and why. We may agree with the thesis of Ian Steele's 1990 book *Betrayals*—that a series of betrayals caused a siege and surrender to deteriorate into a massacre—nevertheless, we do not know whether this was the result of deliberate treachery on the part of the French commander, the Marquis de Montcalm (see the box "The Marquis de Montcalm"), or that Montcalm was merely helpless to control his Indian allies. We disagree just as strongly on the issue of whether the British commander in Fort Edward, Major General Daniel Webb, could or should have sent reinforcements from Fort Edward to help the besieged garrison on Lake George. What appears as a general's cowardice to some is viewed as necessary self-preservation by others. And there is a host of specific points about which the documents do not give clear answers. For example, how many soldiers were actually killed during the siege? How many men, women, and children were butchered during the massacre that followed? Where did the massacre take place, and can the site be found and excavated?

Controversy, of course, even surrounds the present reconstruction of Fort William Henry. Modern visitors to the fort that was rebuilt in the 1950s constantly ask whether it was accurately re-created and on precisely the correct site. Does a vast cemetery of hundreds of soldiers' bodies underlie the fort's parking lot, vulnerable to future development? And if so, is it ethical or appropriate for scientists to disturb these skeletons or display them to the public? For many historical questions, there are no best answers, and controversy will continue to provide visitors with reasons to keep returning to this sandy promontory overlooking Lake George. Like us, future generations will no doubt wonder whether death was unavoidable for the unfortunate soldiers who served the British monarchy on the northern frontier.

★ The Marquis de Montcalm

Louis Joseph, Marquis de Montcalm-Gozon de Saint-Veran (1712–1759), was easily the most brilliant and controversial French military leader in eighteenth-century America. Born near Nîmes in the south of France, he joined the French army at the age of fifteen, received a captaincy at seventeen, and saw distinguished service in several military campaigns on the Continent. His bravery and devotion to church and king led to his appointment by Louis XV to command the armies of France in America. In April of 1756, newly appointed to the rank of major-general, Montcalm set sail for Canada and soon arrived in Quebec City, from which he was to lead French forces against the much more populous English colonies.

As Ticonderoga came under threat of attack from the English, Montcalm traveled there in the summer of 1756 and then on to Oswego in western New York, where he defeated and burned three English forts and took some sixteen hundred prisoners. Some of the captives were killed by Canadians and Indians under his command, an unfortunate event that was repeated the following August as Montcalm led ten thousand soldiers and Indians in the successful attack upon Fort William Henry. For such a "massacre" of prisoners and civilians to have occurred twice points out the difficulty that Montcalm faced when leading diverse forces that were sometimes intent upon plunder. There has been endless speculation and debate as to whether Montcalm could have done more to prevent the slaughter.

In spite of this controversy, there is no denying that Montcalm achieved his greatest success in 1758, when he successfully directed the defense of Fort Ticonderoga against an overwhelming British and Provincial force of ten thousand. But his frequent successes and the

The Marquis de Montcalm. © Bettman/CORBIS.

unquestioned loyalty of his men could not withstand forever the superior numbers of English soldiers who increasingly brought pressure upon New France. In September 1759, Montcalm was mortally wounded on the Plains of Abraham outside Quebec City as General Wolfe's army broke through the French lines. It was fitting that Montcalm died in one of the final battles of the French and Indian War, embodying as he did the courage and resolve with which French forces attempted to maintain their colonies in the New World.

The French and Indian Wars

The events that culminated in the destruction of Fort William Henry in 1757 were the outcome of many years of conflict in North America between the French and British colonies. Each European superpower sought to make the North American continent its own, and all of northern New York State was a battleground between the late 1600s and the 1750s. In the first of many struggles, the stockaded settlement of Schenectady on the Mohawk River was attacked and destroyed on February 8, 1690, by about two hundred French Canadians and Indians. Those who were not murdered in their beds were dragged north to captivity in Canada. During the wars that followed—now known as King William's War, Queen Anne's War, and King George's War—towns throughout New England were repeatedly subjected to raids. In the most famous event of Queen Anne's War, the Connecticut River community of Deerfield, Massachusetts, was attacked by Indians and Frenchmen on February 29, 1704, and 112 captives were herded together and forced to march to Canada. Typically, those settlers who reached Canada were either enslaved or held for ransom, and the English reciprocated with raids of their own. Intermittent hostilities between the French and English led to what is now termed the French and Indian War, or Seven Years' War, between 1754 and 1761. The eventual outcome of these struggles was total victory for the English, putting an end to most of France's claims to the North American continent, but the path to victory included many instances of brutality and death.

While the Seven Years' War was very much an international struggle between England and France, its local manifestation within the American colonies, the French and Indian War, began as a battle over territory and trade in western Virginia. In one of his very few defeats, a young George Washington was forced to surrender on July 3, 1754, to a French force from Fort Duquesne after a brief battle at Fort Necessity, a temporary round stockade thrown up by Washington's Virginia militia. Hostilities escalated just a short distance away with the Battle of the Wilderness, or Braddock's Defeat, on July 9, 1755. When Edward Braddock led his Redcoats and Virginians to their deaths near Fort Duquesne, this marked the beginning of a lengthy series of British military failures along the western borders of Virginia, Maryland, and Pennsylvania.

British fortunes were somewhat more successful along the waterways on the eastern side of New York State, where the French had commenced construction of Fort St. Frederic in Crown Point in the year 1734. All of Lake Champlain and Lake George, termed Lac du St. Sacrement by the French, had already been claimed for New France

FIG. 1.2. *Battle of Lake George, NY. September, 1755*. Painted by F. C. Yohn. Courtesy of Chapman Historical Museum.

when the British began to spread north from Albany, creating small, stockaded forts along the Hudson River. One of the outcomes of this confrontation was the savage Battle of Lake George fought on September 8, 1755, between French forces led by Baron Dieskau and a British army led by Major General William Johnson (see fig. 1.2). The British controlled the battlefield at the end of the day, but they had lost two of their principal leaders: Colonel Ephraim Williams, commander of the Massachusetts troops, and King Hendrick, chief of the Mohawks. Later that same day, in the most infamous part of the battle, about two hundred French and Indians were killed and thrown into a nearby pond, known since then as Bloody Pond because of the blood slick that floated on the water for weeks afterward.

Dieskau was wounded and captured during the battle, and his men were thrown back to Fort St. Frederic. After the battle was over, Johnson authorized the construction of Fort William Henry and Fort Edward, both designed by his brilliant chief engineer, William Eyre of the 44th Regiment of Foot. That same month, the French began construction of

Fort Carillon overlooking the portage between Lake Champlain and the outlet from Lake George. Thus began a two-year standoff between opposing forces at the two ends of Lake George. The only direct confrontation occurred on March 19, 1757, when an army of about 1,600 French Regulars, Canadians, and Indians, led by François-Pierre de Rigaud de Vaudreuil, crossed Lake George on the ice and attacked Fort William Henry; however, they had no artillery with them and were easily repulsed.

Still, there was ample military activity elsewhere, especially in western New York State where two small English forts were captured at Oswego on Lake Ontario in August 1756. In a startling development, with implications for what was later to occur at Fort William Henry, about a hundred captives from Fort Oswego and Fort George were slaughtered by Indians on the French side. The leader of French forces at Oswego was a young officer, the Marquis de Montcalm, who was destined to be remembered as one of the bravest yet most controversial figures of the French and Indian War.

The Construction of Fort William Henry

Early British forts were little more than square palisades, vertical logs set into ditches, sometimes surrounded by earthworks or a moat. They lacked the sophistication of French fortifications and were designed to withstand Indian attacks but not artillery bombardments. In response to the French threat from Canada, William Eyre became the first to build a British fort with earth-filled log walls, a glacis, and four diamond-shaped corner bastions like those employed by the French (see the box "French Fort Design"). The walls of Fort William Henry were thirty feet thick, with a core of beach sand packed in between the two log faces. This would be effective in absorbing the impact of cannon fire but would not deter mortar shells lobbed over the walls.

Inside the fort, the central parade ground was surrounded by four log barracks, all of which were two stories high with exterior staircases; those on the east and west also had one story below ground. A powder magazine was built underneath the northeast bastion, a hospital at the southeast corner of the parade, and officers' quarters in small buildings at either end of the East Barracks.

The fort was encircled by a dry moat, or ditch, on three sides, containing a single line of stockade posts or pickets, and by a slope running downhill toward Lake George on the east. Access into the fort was possible only by crossing a bridge that spanned the moat. Contemporary maps (see fig. 1.1) and illustrations on powder horns reveal soldiers' gar-

★ French Fort Design

The French were without peer in the art of fortification. French engineers, most notably Sebastien Le Prestre Vauban (1632–1707), successfully applied the latest scientific principles as they created sturdy fortifications that took advantage of the natural terrain, even as they ensured that every part of a fortification was built within sight of another wall or bastion. To catch your attackers in a cross-fire was thus the defining principle that made French forts successful. The many Vauban-style forts along the Richelieu River, Lake Champlain, and Lake George were not as large as the more permanent coastal fortifications, such as Fortress Louisbourg in Nova Scotia, but nevertheless they were the product of many years of experimentation and innovation in Europe.

Details varied slightly with each fortification, but a typical French fortress was constructed as a square with bastions at each corner, with curtain walls in between, and with one or more *demilunes* (*ravelins*) forward from the walls to protect the curtains. The whole was surrounded by a deep ditch, or moat, from which dirt had been taken to form the massive earthen walls, or ramparts. An attacking soldier thus had to traverse an obstacle course. He began by running up a glacis (a gently sloping earthwork), dropping down into the bottom of the ditch, and then ascending twenty feet or more to get to the top of the rampart, all the while being fired upon from several directions at once. It is small wonder that the best French designers of forts were also adept at directing sieges—they knew better than anyone else how best to breach the walls of a Vauban-style fort.

English forts were crude in comparison, consisting of little more than earthen embankments and log palisade walls, typically enclosing a central parade ground. And so it was with good reason that the English began to emulate the French style of fortification, beginning with Fort William Henry and Fort Edward in 1755 and followed in 1759 by His Majesty's Fort at Crown Point. Successive English log forts employed corner bastions and were surrounded by dry moats, just like the French forts, ensuring that it would now be much more difficult for an attacker to reach the walls.

dens on the north and west, a privy or "necessary" at the northeast corner of the fort that jutted out over the water, and a very large swamp to the south. The fort itself was small and could have held no more than 400–500 soldiers and officers. Consequently, the bulk of the British force, about 1,800 men, occupied an entrenched camp on a rocky hilltop about 750 yards to the southeast, the same spot where the Battle of Lake George had earlier been fought.

William Eyre was made the first commander of Fort William Henry, and the flag was raised on November 13, 1755. Eyre's garrison included British Regulars and two companies of Rogers' Rangers. Although the fort itself was unusually well built, some sources suggest that life at the fort was increasingly dirty and disease-ridden, especially among the Provincial soldiers. In a 1756 letter, Lieutenant-Colonel Ralph Burton wrote that there were

> about 2,500 men, 500 of them sick, the greatest part of them what they call poorly. They bury from five to eight daily, and officers in proportion. Extremely indolent and dirty to a degree the fort stinks enough to cause an infection.

Poor sanitary conditions, coupled with a high rate of smallpox, suggest that everyday life inside the fort was characterized by high levels of sickness and death, greatly reducing the readiness of the garrison. This was by no means unusual for a Provincial camp at that time, but Burton's statement also reflects the contempt with which Regular British officers viewed their colonial counterparts.

The Siege and Massacre

By mid-1757, command of the fort had been given to a Scotsman, Lieutenant-Colonel George Monro of the 35th Regiment of Foot. Monro was a career officer, with three reputed children in Ireland, all minors. As reports reached the British of an imminent French attack, he was sent reinforcements in the form of Massachusetts Provincials, New York Provincials, and the 60th (Royal American) Regiment. Still, this left Monro with a total garrison of only about 2,372 men, many of whom were sickly, accompanied by some family members and camp followers.

In August 1757, a vastly superior army of at least eight thousand French and Indians advanced upon Fort William Henry, having left Fort Carillon on July 30; the exact size of the French force has been much-debated, and estimates have been made as high as ten to fourteen thousand. Most of the army traveled in boats, although about three thousand soldiers had marched down the west side of Lake George, and the Indians had journeyed by their own trails. The French were led by the Marquis de Montcalm, and their 1,600 Indian allies were drawn from some thirty-three tribes, scattered from the Great Lakes all across eastern Canada. Although Monro hoped for additional reinforcements from Fort Edward, where about 2,500 Regulars and militia waited in reserve, Major General Daniel Webb was unwilling to risk the remainder of his soldiers against a larger force in the forest. The French were well armed with cannons, which they had floated on rafts down the lake, and they established positions and cannon batteries on points of high ground on the west side of the lake. The fort was surrounded and escape cut off, and the bombardment began on the third of August. Siege trenches were extended each night, dug by Canadian militia, bringing French artillery closer to their targets each day.

It required only six days of shelling before Monro surrendered the fort, and there are several surviving accounts of the siege. Jabez Fitch Jr., listening to the action while at his post in Fort Edward, was one of those who gave daily progress reports:

> [August 3]: I Hered ye Morning Gun Fire at ye Lake Before ours—a little after Sun Rise we Here he [*sic*] Cannon Fire Briskly at ye Lake and also ye Small arms we Immediately Contluded [*sic*] that they were At-tacted—This Firing Lasted Most of ye Day.
>
> [August 4]: I Hear By ye Prisoner that Colyar Brought in that the French Have Got a Vary Strong army against Fort Wm Henry He Said there was 6000 Ragulars & 5000 Canadians.
>
> [August 5]: Before Sunrise We Heard ye Canon Play Vary Brisk at ye Lake Soon after ye Small arms Began to Fire this Firing Lasted all Day with-out Much Ceasing it was Contluded that this Day there was ye Most Ammunition Expended that Ever was in a Day at that Plais Before.
>
> [August 9]: We Had a Rumer about Noon that Fort Wm Henry was Taken for their Firing Seasd Some Time in ye Morning.

Jabez Fitch, like many of the other soldiers waiting in Fort Edward, wanted to go to the rescue of his comrades, but the orders were never given.

During the several-day siege, many of the British cannons and mor-tars exploded because of metal fatigue, and spirits inside the fort must have deteriorated as the siege trenches advanced toward them. The loss of artillery was extremely serious, and *The New-Hampshire Gazette* noted, on August 22: "And they having burst their 32 Pounders, two 18 pound-ers, two 12 Pounders, 2 nine Pounders, and two Brass Mortars, and but 17 Shells left, they concluded to hoist the white Flag, which Montcalm answered" (p. 2). The same problem was touched on by Jabez Fitch Jr., who wrote on August 5: "But we Understand that this Morning ye En-imy Had Not Got their artilery to Bair Upon them—also that our Men had Burst their Largest Morter & one 18 Pounder" (p. 17).

Perhaps the best eyewitness account of the failure of the artillery is that of Colonel Joseph Frye, who led a Massachusetts regiment during the siege of Fort William Henry. According to Frye, on August 4 they "burst a mortar"; on the fifth they "burst Two 32 pounders and one 18 pounder"; on the sixth they "burst One 18 pounder & One 12 pounder and . . . one of our Brass Six pounders"; on the seventh "we Burst One 12 and one 6 pounder"; and on the ninth "we had the misfortune to burst another mortar." Also on August 9, Frye recorded that the only functional artillery left in the fort consisted of two six-pounders, one nine-pounder, two four-pounders, one seven-inch mortar, and one seven-inch howitzer. This simply was not enough artillery with which to mount a credible defense, and the fort was also running out of shot and shells.

The British officers held a final meeting on August 9, at which time they agreed there was no hope of relief from Fort Edward. The French siege trenches were now so close—they had been dug for 890 yards—that there was no choice but to surrender to Montcalm. The terms of surrender, the Articles of Capitulation, required the soldiers to leave the fort on August 9, but they were allowed to keep their personal belongings and weapons, though without any ammunition. As a gesture of respect for their gallant defense, Montcalm also allowed the British to take one cannon with them. The men were required to pledge that they would not fight against the French for at least the next eighteen months. They would march, with an escort of about 450 French Regulars, to their sister base at Fort Edward, fifteen miles away, while the sick and injured would remain inside Fort William Henry.

The terms were generous, partially because the French were low on food and didn't want to feed so many prisoners, but it was now almost impossible for the Indians to obtain the scalps or captives they sought. Immediately after the surrender, as the garrison left the fort, some of the Indians attached to Montcalm's army dashed inside the fort and killed and scalped roughly seventeen sick and wounded British soldiers, as well as some women and children. Other Indians dug up the fort's cemetery to steal redcoats and blankets from the bodies, and in the process they scalped the dead, many of whom had died from smallpox (see the box "Who Invented Scalping?").

On August 10, some of the Indians assaulted the entrenched camp, and then the Abenakis attacked the rear of the column of soldiers and families as they started down the military road toward Fort Edward (see fig. 1.3). What started as an effort to steal clothing and rum from the soldiers quickly escalated into an unrestrained frenzy of killing and scalping, and hundreds of prisoners were seized who could be taken to Canada to be held for ransom. It is unclear exactly where this took place, and it is also uncertain whether the escort of French Regulars did anything to protect their prisoners during their march. Certainly they did not do enough. It *is* clear that Colonel Monro and his senior officers were not with the unarmed column. Instead, Monro and other British officers were taken to the French camp, where they were held until after the fort was leveled. Monro was then escorted on horseback,

★ Who Invented Scalping?

Scalping was one of the most terrifying customs in the American colonies, one of the most unforgettable threats to safety on the frontier. This was an ancient practice in many Native American cultures, and cuts and scratches found on skulls in Indian graves demonstrate that scalping was widespread for a thousand years or more. There is no evidence for this custom ever having been practiced in Europe, although the Europeans did not lack for objectionable practices of their own, such as beheading, hanging, and disemboweling. Originally one of the reasons for removing the scalp with a knife or ax appears to have been to release the soul from the victim's body, but the primary reason was no doubt to obtain an easily portable trophy. In the colonial period this custom was exacerbated due to European intervention: James Axtell and William Sturtevant have pointed out that the French urged the Indian scalping of whites, and the English encouraged the white scalping of Indians. Both European nations offered rewards or bounties for scalps and clearly contributed to scalping's becoming even more pervasive. Curiously enough, it was not uncommon for a victim to survive the scalping, to regrow some of the missing skin, and to live a long life afterward. Still, scalping left permanent traces behind, including scar tissue and lesions on the bone.

Scalping typically enabled young braves to take home with them tangible evidence of their courage and success in battle, and this was much easier to do than carrying with them the heads of their enemies. Once the scalps were dried and displayed next to a warrior's lodge, they were clear proof of his valor and his worthiness to be a husband and leader. Procuring scalps was thus one of the main goals of the Canadian Indians who attacked the column of soldiers and civilians as they retreated down the military road to Fort Edward. After all, the surrender of British forces at Fort William Henry was on terms that would have prevented the Indians from obtaining the trophies that they so eagerly sought to take home with them to Canada.

One of the skeletons recovered from Fort William Henry reveals clear signs of scalping along the edge of the hairline, but it is likely that many others at the fort suffered the same fate. Richard Rogers, a Ranger and brother of Major Robert Rogers, was already dead and buried in the cemetery at the time he was scalped. Major Israel Putnam, writing after the massacre, described how "Dead bodies, mangled with scalping-knives and tomahawks in all the wantonness of Indian fierceness and barbarity, were every where to be seen." Jabez Fitch Jr., waiting in nearby Fort Edward, tells us how "the Savages Plunderd Stript Kild & Scalpt our People." It may be a dubious distinction, but the scalping that occurred at Fort William Henry contributed greatly to its image as a site of horror.

FIG. 1.3. *Surrender of Fort William Henry, Lake George, N.Y. August 1757.* Painted by J. L. G. Ferris. Courtesy of Chapman Historical Museum.

accompanied by about five hundred soldiers, wives, and others, back to Fort Edward on August 15. They transported with them the solitary six-pound cannon that was to have been the symbol of their honorable surrender.

Contemporary sources provide extremely graphic accounts of the violence that took place on the road. Jabez Fitch Jr. wrote in his diary

> ye Indians Beset our People & Kild them with their Speers Robd them of all that they were allowed by ye Capitulation. Children they took from their Mothers & Dasht their Brains out against ye Stons ye Mothers they Servd ye Same and also their Husbands if they offerd to Relieve them So.

Colonel Joseph Frye, who was actually there in the midst of the massacre and barely escaped with his life, described how at the entrenched camp the Indians

> began to take the Officers Hatts, Swords, Guns & Cloaths, Striping them all to their Shirts, and on some officers Left no Shirt at all. While this was

doing they Killd & Scalpt all the Sick & wounded before our faces, then took out from Our troops, all the Indians and negroes and Carried them off. One of the former they burnt alive afterwards.

Once the column of retreating soldiers and civilians had finally started down the military road, Frye described how the Indians fell upon the rear of the column and began carrying away

Officers, privates, Women & Children, Some of which Latter they killed & Scalp'd in the Road. This horrid Scene of Blood & Slaughter Obliged our Officers to apply to the Officers of the French guard for protection, which they refused, and told them, they must take to the Woods, and Shift for themselves, which many did.

It was chiefly New Hampshire soldiers and some of the camp followers who were at the end of the column and who took the brunt of the attack.

Newspaper articles and soldiers' and officers' journals in the 1750s naturally stressed the atrocities that followed the surrender of Fort William Henry, but they exaggerated the number of those killed and captured by the attacking French and Indian force. Estimates of those slain ranged as high as 1,500, and early authors placed great emphasis on the wanton slaughter of women and children, no doubt to incite larger numbers of British settlers ("militia") to enlist against the French. Jabez Fitch Jr. was told that during the siege "we Had about 50 Men Kild" but that during the massacre that followed, "ye Slaughter of this Day is Soposd to Be Vastly Greater than all the Rest."

While we do not know the exact number killed, a modern analysis of the massacre by historian Ian Steele in his book *Betrayals* suggests that the total number killed may have been only about 185; he further argues that the killing of the British switched over fairly quickly to the taking of prisoners, viewed as "property" by the Indians. Steele bases his estimate on the number of those who actually surrendered on August 9— 2,308 men and perhaps 148 family members and camp followers—relative to those who later escaped to safety in Fort Edward. While Steele's estimate appears exceptionally low when compared to early sources, he nevertheless has carefully researched all available documents.

It is clear that a majority of the fleeing English soldiers escaped, although many had lost their belongings and even their clothing. Montcalm was personally instrumental in obtaining the release of about four hundred others who were already in Indian hands. Nevertheless, about two hundred were taken to Canada, where they were eventually ransomed or sold into slavery. These conditions made it extremely difficult to determine exactly how many were killed, because some of those who were captured were not ransomed until many months later.

The British were understandably outraged as they described the massacre, but French responses were more ambivalent. Montcalm had given his word that the prisoners would be protected, so the actions of the Indians were a severe blow to his reputation and honor. Montcalm's personal aide, Captain Louis Antoine de Bougainville, had written in his journal on August 9: "The chiefs agreed to everything and promised to restrain their young men," but he also noted, "We will be most fortunate if we can avoid a massacre." Later, after the massacre, Bougainville wrote: "Will they in Europe believe that the Indians alone have been guilty of this horrible violation of the capitulation?"

A French Jesuit who accompanied Montcalm's army, Père Pierre Roubaud, was clearly horrified as he wrote, "I saw one of these barbarians come forth out of the casements . . . carrying in his hand a human head, from which streams of blood were flowing, and which he paraded as the most valuable prize he had been able to seize." At times, Père Roubaud attempted to put an end to some of the atrocities, but it is clear that the French had little control over their Indian allies, and many were absolutely horrified at the brutality they witnessed. In perhaps the best known example of this, one of the English prisoners who was taken to Canada was killed by Indians, and Bougainville described in his journal how they "put him in a kettle, and forced his unfortunate compatriots to eat him."

After the surrender, the French prepared a detailed listing of the stores and weapons that they seized inside the fort. Removing what they wanted, they burned and dismantled the fort between August 11 and 15, leveling the charred timbers by hand. Instead of proceeding on to attack Fort Edward, Montcalm returned with his forces to Fort Carillon (Ticonderoga), thirty-five miles to the north, and most of the army then went back to Canada for the winter. The Indians returned to their villages, carrying smallpox with them and unknowingly causing the deaths of thousands of their own people.

Sadly, Colonel Monro, who had survived the ordeal and was safely returned to Fort Edward, died just three months later in East Greenbush, a suburb of Albany. He had traveled to Albany in late August or early September; he died "on the street" on November 3 and was buried in what is now St. Peter's Episcopal Church in Albany. James Austin Holden, writing in 1917, has noted that "his death was attributed to apoplexy," and "Evidently he brooded on his sorrows and lack of governmental support till both took their toll of body and mind." The fall of Fort William Henry was definitely not of Monro's choosing, nor was the massacre, and it can be argued that General Webb's inaction contributed greatly to Monro's demise. Sir William Johnson has provided what is probably the harshest assessment of Webb, whom he bluntly characterized "as the only Englishman he ever knew who was a coward."

From 1757 to 1952

Events at Fort William Henry had been unusually violent, and the British chose not to rebuild the fort after visiting the charred ruins a few days later. Revenge was paramount in the minds of the English, and General Abercromby camped on the spot in 1758, before unsuccessfully attacking Fort Carillon. In 1759, Lord Jeffrey Amherst constructed Fort George on the high ground at the south end of the lake, even as some of his men camped atop the ruins of Fort William Henry. With the fall of Fort Carillon in July of that year, British armies shifted their attention away from Lake George and north to Canada, where Quebec City fell that September and then Montreal in 1760. Only Fort George continued to be occupied within the community of Lake George, although smallpox hospitals were erected on top of the remains of Fort William Henry during the American Revolution.

Historians throughout the nineteenth century were unceasing in their condemnation of the French and Indians. The great midcentury historian, Benson Lossing, was especially colorful in his description of the massacre:

> The savages, two thousand warriors in number, were enraged at the terms of capitulation, for they were induced to serve in this expedition by a promise of plunder. This was denied them, and they felt at liberty to throw off all restraint. As soon as the last man left the gate of the fort, they raised the hideous war-whoop, and fell upon the English with the fury of demons. The massacre was indiscriminate and terrible, and the French were idle spectators of the perfidy of their allies. They refused interference, withheld the promised escort, and the savages pursued the poor Britons with great slaughter, half way to Fort Edward. Fifteen hundred of them were butchered or carried into hopeless captivity. Montcalm utterly disclaimed all connivance, and declared his inability to prevent the massacre without ordering his men to fire upon the Indians.

Later, in his monumental *Montcalm and Wolfe*, published in 1884, Francis Parkman all but exonerated the French for what had taken place, placing all blame squarely on the Indians, whom he constantly compared to "wolves" in his writings.

Still, no historian had an impact equal to that of James Fenimore Cooper, who successfully personalized the events on Lake George in his novel *The Last of the Mohicans*, first published in 1826. By viewing the siege of Fort William Henry through the eyes of Natty Bumppo, a Provincial scout, Cooper created an image of the battle that has transcended and ultimately replaced reality. Later authors, such as Mark

Twain and James Austin Holden, attacked Cooper for his historical inaccuracies, but it is Cooper's version of the massacre that will always be best remembered.

While historians may have been steadfast in damning the tragic events at Fort William Henry, the site itself began to change. In 1854 a truly grand summer resort, the Fort William Henry Hotel, opened just north of the fort site, in the area where soldiers once had their gardens (see fig. 1.4). The hotel thrived until 1908, when it was destroyed by fire, but it was quickly rebuilt by the owner, the Delaware & Hudson Railroad Company. The second Fort William Henry Hotel opened on the same site in 1911, smaller and much less grand (see fig. 1.5). The bastions of the fort remained untouched, although heavily overgrown with pine trees, and visitors from the resort hotels often strolled through the ruins, no doubt drawn by the site's ambiance and reputation (see fig. 1.6). One of the best descriptions of the fort during this period was prepared by James Austin Holden in 1917:

> At Lake George the ruins of Fort William Henry and Fort George, their trenches and walls overgrown with turf and evergreens, their slopes grassed and concealed by underbrush, remain mute reminders of a day long since gone by. . . . So peaceful and so serene the scene, we who visit there scarce can visualize the scenes of blood and carnage, of disaster and death, which once marred these sylvan camps.

FIG. 1.4. Postcard view of the "New Fort Wm. Henry Hotel, Lake George, N.Y.," © 1905. Courtesy of the Village of Lake George.

FIG. 1.5. Postcard view of the "Fort Wm. Henry Hotel, on Lake George, N.Y." Mailed in 1930. Courtesy of the Village of Lake George.

FIG. 1.6. "Site of Old Fort William Henry, Lake George, N.Y." The surface of Fort William Henry in 1910. Reproduced from the Collections of the Library of Congress.

FIG. 1.7. Visitors touring the 1950s excavation, at the site of the Northwest Bastion. Fort William Henry Museum.

This appearance did not change until 1952, ensuring that the foundations would be exceptionally well preserved.

From the 1950s to the Present

In 1952 a group of businessmen headed by Harold Veeder, a real estate broker, concluded that the site of Fort William Henry had the potential to become a remarkable tourist attraction, able to tell one of the most controversial stories of eighteenth-century America. Veeder and his associates purchased the ruins, formed the Fort William Henry Corporation, and commenced the archeology that was needed to reconstruct the fortifications and interior buildings. Given the public's love for a stirring tale of murder and mayhem and after successive retellings of the story for two hundred years, the time was finally right to dig into the charred, sand-covered remains of the fort and to rebuild a full-sized replica that visitors could walk through, admire, and learn from (see fig. 1.7).

Many other forts had been re-created before this one, but few as accurately. Copies of British construction plans drafted in 1755 helped to define its appearance, and excavations by archeologist Stanley Gifford helped to locate the original footprint of the fort (see the box "Stanley Gifford, the Indiana Jones of His Day"). Gifford was assisted by his wife Ruth and a team of college-age men, none of whom had done archeology

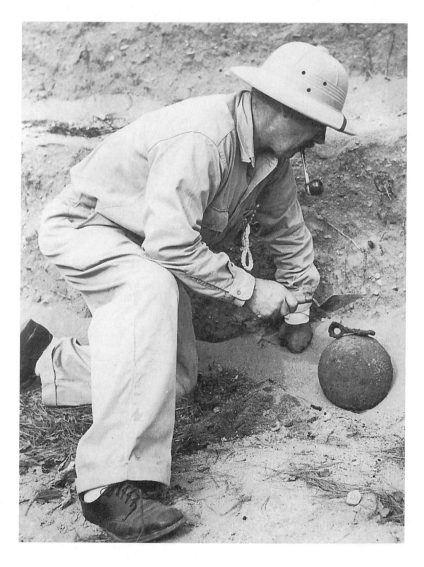

FIG. 1.8. An unexploded mortar shell, with an ax stuck to it, was discovered in a pit in the East Barracks in 1955. Fort William Henry Museum.

★ Stanley Gifford, the Indiana Jones of His Day

Many archeologists like to cultivate the image of being rather impetuous and irascible. Stanley Gifford, the first excavator of Fort William Henry, was no exception. After all, the public expects us to have all of the hell-raising qualities of an Indiana Jones! Before arriving at Fort William Henry, "Stan" had worked as an assistant archeologist for the Heye Foundation in New York City, as curator at Fort Ticonderoga, and as museum director for the Onondaga Historical Association in Syracuse. While it has been 45 years since Stan opened up his trenches at Fort William Henry, he and his wife, Ruth, are fondly remembered by the owners of the fort and others in Lake George who knew him. Stan was a competent digger for his day, especially given the severe time and money constraints he was working under, but he was also a bit of a "wild man," if the stories are to be believed.

Probably the most frequently told story about Stan describes the evening in 1956 that a group of sponsors and investors decided to hold a party at the fort, only to be interrupted by a gun-toting Stan who ordered everyone off "his" site because he felt they weren't being properly respectful! Luckily he was disarmed of his "trusty '38" without shots being fired, but Stan was protective and a bit feisty by nature. And that was especially true when anyone dared to look twice at Ruth!

Many photographs have survived that show Stan in his felt hat and khakis, carrying his "war bag" (a World War II duffle bag that contained his revolver), with a pipe dangling from his mouth, looking every inch like a slightly-balding Indiana Jones. He was often frustrated by having to dig so quickly in advance of construction and by having to show tourists the *same* artifacts over and over. Stan lectured widely about his findings

Stanley Gifford using a modified World War II mine detector to locate cannonballs. Fort William Henry Museum.

at Fort William Henry, was featured in countless magazine and newspaper stories, and afterwards produced a popular-style booklet about the history of the fort. Still, he died only a few years later, in 1961, and there was no final publication of his findings. Most of his excavation records have disappeared, leaving nothing but photographs and a few small field notebooks for the current generation of archeologists to use as a guide while digging at the fort.

I often wish that I could have met Stan and compared notes with him about where to dig next. Our archeological techniques would be a bit different, given the improvements in field methods over the years, but there would certainly be a bond between us given our shared love for uncovering the past. It would be just like meeting the "real" Indiana Jones!

before, and their trenching through the sandy ruins began in the spring of 1953 and lasted through 1954. Working on a very tight schedule, just ahead of the construction crew, Gifford focused especially upon the foundation of the northwest bastion, the corner of the fort that had received the most direct bombardment from the French. To determine original ground and floor levels, he also dug the center of the parade ground, part of the moat, rooms inside the foundations of the East and West Barracks buildings, and part of the cemetery outside the southwest corner of the fort (see figs. 1.8, 1.9, 1.10, and 1.11). Gifford discovered human skeletons throughout the ruins, and the bones in the cemetery revealed scalp marks and other types of trauma.

The archeologists worked just barely ahead of the crew of stout Canadian loggers who were rebuilding the fort. Contemporary photo-

FIG. 1.9. A demolition squad from Fort Jay in New York Harbor (542d Ordnance Detachment, Explosive Ordnance Disposal Control) deactivated the mortar shell (fig. 1.10) by emptying the black powder. Fort William Henry Museum.

FIG. 1.10. "Excavations into the site of the East Barracks in 1954 revealed, at a depth of about eight feet, what was believed to be remains of the fort's blacksmith shop. The excavators are viewing some of the artifacts that were exposed there" (*Albany Times-Union*, August 29, 1954). Charred logs from the East Barracks are visible in the background. Fort William Henry Museum.

graphs suggest that the excavation was a nightmare for Gifford's crew because the fort had been built atop fine beach sand, and the pits constantly caved in as sand "flowed" into the holes. Another problem was the tourists, who demanded to see every discovery that the archeologists made. A few years ago, a middle-aged woman described to us how she had been an eight-year-old girl when her parents took her to visit the dig at Fort William Henry. Again and again she had run underneath the rope barrier to "help" the archeologists, and each time they had shooed her away. Finally, they gave up and handed her a brush with which she contentedly cleaned off a buried bottle. It was the thrill of her life.

As money for archeology ran out, the construction crew rebuilt most of the fort for what it had initially cost to rebuild just the south wall!

In the years that followed the grand opening in 1955, the only additional archeological project was an unsuccessful effort by the museum's staff to dig the fort's well in 1959–1960. Many of the excavated artifacts went on display inside the fort, although some of the best ones were destroyed in 1967 when an arsonist set fire to the West Barracks.

Since 1955, Fort William Henry has been visited by a few million tourists and historians, many of whom have either read or seen a movie version of *The Last of the Mohicans*. From seventy to eighty thousand visitors arrive each year from many different countries, and the reconstructed fort often becomes their first introduction to the French and Indian War. Uniformed interpreters, exhibits within the barracks buildings, a "grenadier bomb-toss," a whipping post, and guided tours all are

FIG. 1.11. Some of the artifacts found in the blacksmith shop included "nine hewing axes, a Rangers' tomahawk, a 24-pound cannonball, a shovel, heavy iron bar of the type used as cannon axles, a copper lead ladle for bullet making, and several finished pieces of iron work used on the cannon and cannon cartridges" (*Albany Times-Union*, August 29, 1954). Fort William Henry Museum.

used to tell the story of Fort William Henry. Many of the early visitors to the fort were well aware of the site's history, and some had ancestors who had fought there. Increasingly, though, modern audiences have no personal connection to the fort, no ancestors who lived in America in the eighteenth century, and no formal education in the colonial wars. It is definitely a challenge for visitors to absorb the reasons for the French and Indian War, hear the story of the "massacre," and to see the exhibits and reconstructed buildings, all within the space of about two hours.

Chapter 2

The Last of the Mohicans, Fact or Fiction?

The Story

THE SIEGE AND MASSACRE that consumed Fort William Henry became one of colonial America's first great tragedies, mixing elements of courage, slaughter, deceit, and dishonor. No wonder that James Fenimore Cooper, already an established author, used the story as the basis for *The Last of the Mohicans*, the second novel in the *Leather-Stocking Tales*, his great saga of the opening of the American frontier (see the box "The Author of the *Leather-Stocking Tales*").

Cooper presents *The Last of the Mohicans* as the story of two British forts, surrounded by endless forest that was impassable to all but the Indians, whose raiding parties often made life unbearable to those who ventured north from Albany. The more southerly fort, where the novel begins, was Fort Edward, a large and relatively secure base on the Hudson River. Fifteen miles to the north was Fort William Henry, a more vulnerable outpost at the southern end of Lake George, occupied by Lieutenant-Colonel George Monro and approximately 2,400 soldiers and civilians (figs. 2.1 and 2.2).

In a rather implausible literary device, Cooper begins his story with the two daughters of Colonel Monro, the fair-haired Alice and the dark-haired Cora, who are attempting to join their father on Lake George. Their timing could not have been more foolish, nor unlikely, because of the threat posed by the French army that is rapidly approaching Fort William Henry. However, we are asked to believe that the colonel's daughters will endure any hardship to be with their father in his time of need. Their escort consists of Major Duncan Heyward, a young British officer who is clearly infatuated with ~~Alice~~ CORA; a psalm-singer, David Gamut; and a Huron guide, Magua.

In setting out from Fort Edward, the small party soon loses its way, thanks to the treachery of Magua, who secretly bears a grudge against

★ The Author of the *Leather–Stocking Tales*

James Fenimore Cooper was born in 1789 in Burlington, New Jersey, and grew up in Cooperstown, New York, a frontier village on Lake Otsego. Cooperstown had been founded by his father, Judge William Cooper, an extremely influential land speculator and congressman. Although he attended Yale College from 1803 to 1805, James was expelled without finishing and went on to become a midshipman in the U.S. Navy. Some years later, Cooper traveled widely in Europe, but he eventually settled back in Cooperstown, where the success of his novels helped him to become one of the most popular writers of the early nineteenth century. It is widely recognized that his experiences in central New York State contributed greatly to the themes and characters in his novels, and his most famous creation, the woodsman Natty Bumppo, alias Leather-Stocking, was most likely based on Nathaniel Shipman, an elderly scout, hunter, and trapper who was well known to Cooper's family. Shipman had been a distinguished Indian fighter during the French and Indian War and often lived with the Mohicans, who respected him greatly. In a sense, then, Hawk-eye was a very real figure, even if he did not actually serve at Fort William Henry.

Although Cooper produced many other writings, the novels that made up the *Leather-Stocking Tales*, published between 1823 and 1841, were his central body of work. *The Deerslayer* and *The Last of the Mohicans*, featuring Natty Bumppo as a young man, are certainly the best-known stories in this series, whereas *The Pathfinder*, *The Pioneers*, and *The Prairie* featured Natty Bumppo at progressively later stages in his life. Although the books sold well, Cooper's family had had financial reversals, and most of the early proceeds from his book sales went to satisfy creditors.

Cooper's best-known novel, *The Last of the Mohicans*, was the result of a visit that Cooper

1822 portrait of James Fenimore Cooper. Fenimore Art Museum, Cooperstown, New York.

paid to Glens Falls in 1825. After he viewed the caverns hollowed out by water in the middle of the Hudson River, that became the spot where Hawk-eye and his traveling companions hid from the Hurons while attempting to reach Fort William Henry. In a novel filled with images of the vast, wild forests of northern New York State, overshadowed by the violence and cruelty displayed by human protagonists, Cooper was so inspired by what is now known as "Cooper's Cave" that it provided him with the impetus to create his greatest story. *The Last of the Mohicans* has lost none of its popularity over the years, as evidenced by several movies, a 1960s television series, and even a Classics Illustrated comic book.

James Fenimore Cooper became a writer in the 1820s at a time when American authors had yet to achieve any commercial success as novelists. His first triumph as a writer was with *The Spy*, the story of an American spy during the Revolutionary War, and he became the first American to write successfully and profitably for a public that had previously considered English authors and books to be more fashionable.

One of the best assessments of Cooper's skills as a writer is that of James Austin Holden, writing in 1917, who observed:

> Those familiar with the life of James Fenimore Cooper will remember the almost instantaneous success of "The Pioneers," which introduced "Natty Bumppo" as a new and distinct type to American and foreign readers of fiction, a character often imitated, but never surpassed or even equaled by novelists since Cooper's day, in the minds of able critics. Probably no greater pen pictures of Indian or backwoodsmen's life have ever been produced than those in the quintette of novels known as the "Leather-stocking Tales," in which Cooper carried his likeable, entertaining, manly and brave hero from virile youth to feeble, decrepit old age.

Cooper died at home in Cooperstown in 1851 but left a powerful legacy as one of America's first truly remarkable authors. He sold many thousands of books during his lifetime, and they have been subsequently translated into a great many languages.

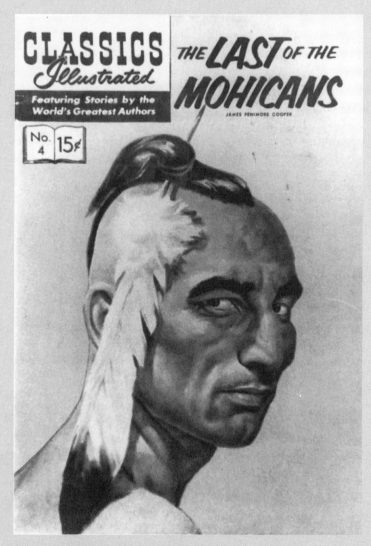

The cover of the Classics Illustrated comic book, *The Last of the Mohicans*.

FIG. 2.1. "A Plan of Fort William Henry. EXPLANATION A. New Barracks for Soldiers. B. New Magazine. CC. Old Barracks. D. Hospital. EE. Sheds for Officers. FF. Provincial Store Houses. GG. Huts built by the Soldiers. H. the ravelin." Courtesy of J. Robert Maguire.

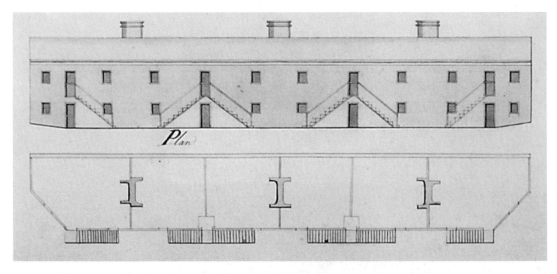

FIG. 2.2. "Elevation of the New Barracks built at Fort William Henry. 1756." Courtesy of J. Robert Maguire.

Colonel Monro. Unknown to his traveling companions, Magua had once served Monro. When he became drunk, Monro had him whipped. Fortunately for the two sisters, they are soon joined by three friends who are wise in the ways of the forest, the white man Natty Bumppo, also known as Hawk-eye, and the Mohican father and son, Chingachgook and Uncas. They are immediately suspicious of Magua's intentions, for he is clearly leading them into a trap. As Magua flees into the forest, Hawk-eye and his two Indian "brothers" deliver the sisters, Heyward, and Gamut to Fort William Henry along forest trails that are alive with hostile Hurons. Along the way, they hide in what is now known as "Cooper's Cave" in Glens Falls (fig. 2.3); they pass by Bloody Pond in Lake George, where Hawk-eye recites the events of 1755 that are now known as the Battle of

FIG. 2.3. A huge painting of Cooper's Cave by Griffith Bailey Coale that hangs in the lobby of the Queensbury Hotel in Glens Falls; it now is reproduced as a postcard.
© Dean Color, Glens Falls, N.Y.

Lake George; and they fight numerous battles with the Indians from Canada who seek to deny them passage to Fort William Henry.

In spite of so many obstacles, the small party finally arrives at Fort William Henry, only to endure the last stages of the siege and surrender of the fort. Cooper's description of the appearance of the fort is rich and colorful:

> Directly on the shore of the lake, and nearer to its western than to its eastern margin, lay the extensive earthen ramparts and low buildings of William Henry. Two of the sweeping bastions appeared to rest on the water . . . while a deep ditch and extensive morasses guarded its other sides and angles. The land had been cleared of wood for a reasonable distance around the work, but every other part of the scene lay in the green livery of nature.

Monro's daughters, Heyward, and Gamut join the retreating garrison as they march down the military road toward Fort Edward, and so they are present at the massacre. Cooper's treatment of this event reflects the prevailing belief of the 1820s that fully 1,500 of the British had been murdered, and he ably describes the horror that must have been felt:

> There arose such a yell along the plain, and through the arches of the wood, as seldom burst from human lips before. They who heard it listened with a curdling horror at the heart, little inferior to that dread which may be expected to attend the blast of the last summons.
> More than 2000 raving savages broke from the forest at the signal and threw themselves across the fatal plain.

Alice, Cora, Heyward, and Gamut survive the massacre but are captured by Magua and his band of Hurons. And so as captives they begin their terrifying journey north toward Canada, feeling revulsion as well as horror because Magua has expressed his personal feelings for Cora, whom he will spare if she agrees to give in to him and share his wigwam. Hawk-eye, Chingachgook, and Uncas follow close behind, eventually catching up to the Hurons and their captives. In the end, Cora and Uncas are killed, as is the vengeful Magua. Chingachgook, now that his son is lost, has truly become "the last of the Mohicans," symbolizing that his people's claims to the land are now fated to pass on to the white man.

James Fenimore Cooper, a Great Storyteller

That, in essence, is the story that Cooper chose to impart to his early-nineteenth-century readers, an audience that probably appreciated tales of courage and terror much more than had their parents because the threat of Indian attack was finally over. No doubt nearly all of Cooper's readers knew which events were real and which were Cooper's literary embellishments, and many unquestionably knew firsthand someone who had served in the colonial wars. Cooper was writing for an extremely knowledgeable audience that probably agreed with his version of American history, at least to the extent that they saw Europe as having "civilized" the wilderness and its Indian population.

Cooper did much to humanize the story of Fort William Henry by peopling it with sympathetic characters, both real and fictional, even if his storytelling has tended to obscure the actual events that occurred at this small English fort. Writing in the 1820s, Cooper reflected the belief of his time that Native people were a mixture of noble savage and bloodthirsty demon. To excite the passions of his readers, Cooper unleashed a torrent of venom upon the Indians, professing them to be sinister, fierce children of the devil, "wily sarpents" [*sic*], treacherous, malignant, barbarous, and more. Clearly, his writings come across as harsh and judgmental to modern readers, but Cooper often attempted to bring out both the good and bad qualities of his eighteenth-century combatants, whether Native, British, or French. For example, while relentlessly criticizing the Canadian Indians who fought alongside Montcalm, Cooper had nothing but praise for the Mohicans, Chingachgook and Uncas, whom he endowed with wisdom, physical perfection, a superb knowledge of the forest, and great personal dignity.

There is no doubt that Cooper reserved the harshest criticisms for the European kings and their local representatives, the military officers, while his most sympathetic protagonists were the English settlers who attempted to pursue normal lives as great events swirled around them. Cooper expressed nothing but contempt for Webb, whom he considered to be a coward for not rushing to the defense of Fort William Henry, and Montcalm was no better for not having restrained his Indian allies and not having protected his prisoners. However, Cooper *did* describe one officer in glowing terms, and that was Colonel Monro, a "resolute Scotsman" who had been betrayed by his superiors.

Appropriately enough, Cooper's greatest admiration was reserved for his own creation, Hawk-eye, one of the new Americans who merely wished to be left alone in his rugged surroundings. The story of Fort William Henry and the massacre truly comes to life in the person of the scout Hawk-eye because this "natural man" of the forest threads his way through events and European military stratagems that would otherwise seem impersonal and of interest only to military historians. Cooper fashions an unusually thorough picture of Hawk-eye, ensuring that readers will be able to visualize him precisely:

The frame of the white man . . . was like that of one who had known hardships and exertion from his earliest youth. . . . He wore a hunting shirt of
forest green, fringed with faded yellow, and a summer cap of skins which
had been shorn of their fur. He also bore a knife in a girdle of wampum . . .
the only part of his underdress which appeared below the hunting frock
was a pair of buckskin leggings that laced at the sides. . . . A pouch and
horn completed his personal accouterments. . . . The eye of the hunter or
scout, whichever he might be, was small, quick, keen, and restless, roving
while he spoke.

While Hawk-eye was, of course, a strictly fictional character, as were
Alice, Cora, Magua, Duncan Heyward, and David Gamut, it was through
the eyes of Hawk-eye that Americans of the new nation were able to
imagine life on the even-earlier frontier, amid images of the darkness of
the forest, the immensity of the American landscape, and the dangers
faced by those who were pawns between the two European superpowers.
And it was only Hawk-eye who managed to maintain his honor and integrity, even as others stumbled under the hardships and dangers of
frontier life.

For Cooper, most Indians were savages who were obsessed with revenge, whereas he characterized the protagonists, the white settlers, as
merry, brave, forgiving, and morally superior by virtue of their Christian
faith. Because Cooper was unquestionably writing a novel, he did not
have to be especially accurate in his character portrayals, and historical
details certainly did not prevent him from telling the story he wanted to
tell. *The Last of the Mohicans* is a rousing good story, full of adventure,
wonderful heroes, and pure evil, personified by the Huron Magua.

There have always been criticisms of Cooper for his artistic license,
most notably "Fenimore Cooper's Literary Offenses" by Mark Twain
(1895) and "The Last of the Mohicans, Cooper's Historical Inventions,
and His Cave" by James Austin Holden (1917). Some of these criticisms
have been petty; for example, Cooper chose the name "Horicon" instead
of "Lake George" for the body of water at the center of his story, and
that was not acceptable to some reviewers. Mark Twain was perhaps the
most outspoken of these, for he disliked *everything* about Cooper's writing style, characterizing it as "singularly dull." In his bluntest assessment
of Cooper's work, Twain also commented that "Cooper wrote about the
poorest English that exists in our language."

No doubt, Cooper was loose with historical facts, and it is sometimes
difficult for modern readers to become used to his wordy and archaic
writing style. Still, it is well worth the investment of time to read and
understand Cooper, because his story is a great one, and he was superb
at developing colorful and exciting characters.

Cooper crafts the story of the massacre in a way that is very different

★ Movies Tell the Story

The Last of the Mohicans has been made into a movie several times, and it is only through the movies that most Americans have come to know this thrilling story. Unfortunately, whenever I ask audiences whether anyone has actually read the entire novel, I often find that many older people have but virtually no one below the age of forty. Yet regardless of age, nearly everyone claims to have watched at least one of the movies of that name.

While the 1992 movie, starring Daniel Day-Lewis as Hawk-eye, "the Long Carabine," is most familiar to modern audiences, it was a remake of a much earlier, 1936 movie featuring Randolph Scott as Hawk-eye and Bruce Cabot as the Huron Magua. Randolph Scott is probably the actor who will always be most closely associated with Hawk-eye—solemn and slow to speak, unbelievably decent and honorable, and definitely the sort of hero with whom you would want to be trapped in the forest. Filmed in black and white by the director George Seitz, the 1936 movie was a superb adventure classic that was commercially successful in its day and is so good that a cut from it is still shown continuously inside a small theater at the reconstructed Fort William Henry. Not as well known is the 1977 film directed by James Conway and starring Steve Forrest as Hawkeye and Ned Romero as Chingachgook. Still, it was well done, and Forrest comes across as a credible "man of the forest."

The latest adventure epic, with Daniel Day-Lewis, improperly named "Nathaniel Poe" instead of Natty Bumppo, is certainly the fastest-paced and most colorful version of this tale. The movie's dark and moody appearance adds gravity to what was unquestionably a very grisly story. Filmed in the Blue Ridge Mountains of North Carolina by the director Michael Mann, none of the scenes looks remotely like the Lake George area; and a brand-new six-million-dollar fort was created for the filming, only to be destroyed afterward. All the same, the forests of North Carolina may well be more authentic-looking for an eighteenth-century story than any stands of timber growing in the Adirondacks today.

While Daniel Day-Lewis is intense and charismatic, a worthy hero by modern standards, there has been much heated debate on the subject of the 1992 movie's inaccuracies, both with respect to Cooper's novel and actual historical fact. The accuracy of all of the movies can easily be attacked because the love stories invariably win out over plot and military stratagems. Perhaps the greatest deceit in the 1992 movie occurs when Colonel Monro is shot and his heart cut out by Magua during the massacre—surely, a gratuitous act since Monro was not even there.

In the 1992 movie, Hawkeye even "wins the girl," Cora, and her sister Alice and Major Heyward are both killed; such fundamental changes in plot surely would not have been pleasing to Cooper. Also, the complex motives that determined how the British, French, and Indians dealt with each other simply are not revealed in any of the movies. These movie characters tend to be either Good or Evil, and such stereotyping about other cultures perhaps contributed to the French and Indian War in the first place. Just as unfortunate is the moviemakers' inability to understand the nature of eighteenth-century technology. The well-known scenes where Hawk-eye is shown running through primeval forest, shooting muskets from the hip with unerring accuracy, are positively hilarious to modern black powder shooters!

Still, the movie versions of *The Last of the Mohicans* have helped to keep alive an interest in the period, thereby communicating a bit of the "feel" of eighteenth-century life to modern viewers.

The movies are perhaps the only way we can appreciate what a bastioned log fort looked like or how British and French soldiers both lined up in formation to fire musket volleys at each other, and we can see how cannons and mortars were fired. It was a gritty life on the American frontier; one hopes that movie viewers will come away with a deeper appreciation of the hardships endured by soldiers and their families. All too often, though, battles and bloody scenes of scalping and throat cutting seem to permeate this type of action film. Inevitably, the strongest memory among moviegoers may be that the French and Indian War was that violent period in American history when everyone collected scalps. After all, that's what we've all seen in the movies!

Daniel Day-Lewis as Hawk-eye in the 1992 movie *The Last of the Mohicans*.

from what modern authors would write, but this demonstrates how the massacre has been redefined by every generation (see the box "Movies Tell the Story"). *The Last of the Mohicans* was very much a product of the 1820s, and Cooper's writing reflects a great deal of outrage and intolerance toward Native people. After all, only sixty-nine years had passed since the massacre, and the events of 1757 were still a very fresh and very emotional topic for most Americans. Cooper was a passionate writer, and in *The Last of the Mohicans* his anger at Webb, Montcalm, and the Indians of Canada is powerful and convincing. Given the facts as he knew them and writing in the language of his day, this was obviously the story that Cooper wanted to tell.

Chapter 3

Modern Archeology at the Fort

Background

STANLEY GIFFORD deserves credit for conducting the first professional archeology in the Lake George area, and he could not have picked a richer or more significant site. After all, Fort William Henry has just about everything that archeologists might dream of: It was the first well-designed British fort in the northern colonies; it gave rise to the most infamous massacre in eighteenth-century America; there was a brief occupation followed by a massive fire, which created a sealed "time capsule" featuring the year 1757; and it is an absolutely beautiful setting in which to work. Beginning in 1953, the dig at Fort William Henry became the largest and certainly the most exciting of the many historic and prehistoric projects that Gifford directed over the course of his career.

While the owners of the fort site tried doing their own small dig in late 1952, it was in 1953 that Gifford was hired to take charge of the full-scale excavation of Fort William Henry. Early on, he set up a motorized sifting machine at the southwest corner of the parade ground, but as one of the diggers on his crew, Carleton Dunn, enjoys remembering, they stopped using the machine when the owners realized that people would actually *pay* to watch the archeologists at work. At the age of twenty, Dunn was the youngest of the diggers, and he still has a superb memory of the details of the project. The same visitors often came back day after day to watch as barracks foundations and thousands of artifacts were unearthed (fig. 3.1). Gifford usually excavated only where one of the structures was about to be rebuilt, typically with a crew of local workmen that did not exceed a half dozen at a time.

Gifford's work focused upon locating the outlines of key buildings, finding the cemetery, which had not been drawn on any historical map, and recovering artifacts that would help in the creation of exciting new exhibits. There was not enough time to expose very many of the fort's foundations and dumps, and this was fortunate because it left some of

FIG. 3.1. Visitors touring the 1950s excavation. Luckily, archeologists no longer dig in white shirts and ties! Fort William Henry Museum.

the ruins untouched, awaiting future generations of archeologists who might wield more refined techniques. After Gifford left Lake George, professional archeology was not attempted at the fort for the next forty years, although many of the visitors must have wondered whether there was a potential for additional discoveries underneath their feet.

I was one of those who wondered whether it would ever again be possible to dig inside the fort. In a fortunate series of coincidences, I was approached in 1996 by Mike Palumbo, then the curator of Fort William Henry, who told me that the owners of the fort were eager to conduct a new series of archeological investigations. Was I interested? At the time, my colleagues and I had been excavating on Rogers Island in Fort Edward since 1991, and by 1996 we had become restless, with too many years spent at a single site. So the answer, of course, was an enthusiastic yes!

Adirondack Community College cheerfully agreed to support the dig, and since then the college has sponsored four summer field schools, enabling us to train many students and volunteers while simultaneously doing our research. Above all, we wanted to learn how accurate the 1950s reconstruction had been and whether past archeologists had left anything intact. The techniques and research questions employed by archeologists have changed a great deal since the 1950s, and we were confident that it would be possible to add a lot to the story of Fort William Henry. Besides, since no records had survived from the previous excavation, it really felt as though we were the *first* ones to dig there.

The first step with any long-term excavation is to create a master grid of permanent reference points over the entire site so that each season our field supervisors can easily add new pits to what has already been excavated. Our surveyors, Gordon and Barbara De Angelo, periodically updated the grid, looking for missing points or extending the grid into new areas where we hadn't previously planned to dig. Initially, we believed that much of our excavation would be conducted *outside* the walls of the reconstructed fort because those areas would not have been disturbed as much during the 1950s. Later, as it became clear that most of the grassy areas around the parking lot and cemetery were heavily disturbed, we devoted much more of our digging time to structural remains inside the walls of the fort. The one exception was the fort's main dump, located just east of the fort, where we kept returning because of its exceptional richness.

Each site received its own number so that artifacts could be analyzed independently of other parts of the fort (see table 3.1).

Archeology inside the Reconstructed Fort

The Northwest Bastion

The northwest bastion was the corner of the fort that received the most direct bombardment from the French during the siege in 1757. In the 1950s, Stanley Gifford focused much of his attention upon this corner of the fort and dug up virtually everything before the bastion was reconstructed. The richness of this area was amazing, and Gifford was able to expose great quantities of mortar shells, cannonballs, and musket balls, many of which went into new exhibits inside the reconstructed fort. Since nothing had been left untouched, this became the one part of the fort where we were unable to do further archeology.

The Parade Ground (Sites 2, 3, 4, 6)

Photographs taken in the 1950s reveal that Gifford dug a huge area in the center of the parade ground, although he often found it impossible

Table 3.1
Sites Excavated at Fort William Henry, 1997–2000

Site	Description	Excavation years
1	Edge of military cemetery	1997, 1998
2	Parade ground, southeast corner	1997
3	Well in parade ground	1997
4	Parade ground, north end	1997
5	Dump east of fort	1997, 1998, 1999
6	Parade ground, south end	1998
7	Parking lot next to Trolley Restaurant	1998
8	West Barracks in parade ground	1998, 1999, 2000
9	Moat surrounding the fort	1999
10	Parking lot (possible breastworks area)	1999
13	Lawn near Tower Theater building	2000

to keep his pit walls vertical in the loose, shifting beach sand. When we started our own work in 1997, we began what developed into four years of challenges and surprises inside the reconstructed fort (fig. 3.2). In some areas we found that the 1750s parade ground lies only about one foot below the surface where tourists walk today; at the other extreme, we sometimes descended for eight feet or more inside the cellars of former buildings. We also found that much of our time was spent shoring up walls with 2-×-8s and sheets of plywood as we tried to prevent the inevitable collapses. It was potentially dangerous work for our diggers; fortunately, the supervisor over most of the workers in the parade ground was Matthew Rozell, a schoolteacher with just the right skills in engineering and carpentry, as well as archeology.

In 1997 we dug several pits in the southeast corner of the parade ground (Site 2) and discovered that Gifford had trenched everywhere, disturbing all of the soil to a depth of seven or eight feet. It was discouraging, and we never went back. Nearby, though, we dug inside the original entranceway into the fort and found eighteenth-century artifacts within a few feet of the present ground level. That was our first indication that the living surface of the fort must have been very close to the modern level.

We also spent both 1997 and 1998 exposing artifacts and looking for evidence of temporary buildings in the northwest corner of the parade (Site 4), between the well and the West Barracks. This area proved to be much richer in artifacts, and there had been only a few soil disturbances. While we found musket balls, pieces of mortar shells, tobacco pipes, and a 1738 Spanish silver real, they were all side by side with prehistoric

FIG. 3.2. Excavations at
the northeast corner of
the parade ground in the
summer of 1997.

artifacts that were in situ (they had not been brought in with fill from
the beach below); this was apparent because we found an intact hearth
and tight clusters of pottery sherds from the same few vessels. This
strongly suggested that very little soil had been deposited over the past
thousand years, between the last prehistoric occupation and the arrival
of the soldiers.

One of our most successful projects inside the parade ground did not
involve buildings or dumps. At the north end of the parade is the fort's
stone-lined well, the center of attention for many of the tourists who
enter the fort. This historic structure had been dug by Rogers' Rangers
in 1756 and had never been a very predictable source of water. In all of
the years after the fort was destroyed, the top of the well had jutted out
of the ruins, often appearing in historical photographs (fig. 1.6). The
upper part was partially excavated in the late 1950s, and then some new
courses of stone were added to the top to make it more visible for tourists.
Ever since 1960, tourists had thrown their own "artifacts" into the well,
ranging from flash cubes to sunglasses, but in 1997 we resolved to plumb
its depths for ourselves, hoping to reach an undisturbed bottom.

I had dug one well before, at Saratoga National Historical Park, and it appeared that the fort's well might present even bigger challenges. Oral history and newspaper accounts from the 1950s claimed that the well might be as much as forty or sixty feet deep. If that were the case, then I would never make it out alive. As it was, weeks of digging took us to the bottom of a thirty-foot-deep well, and no lives were lost. As we descended, the artifacts inside mirrored the changing history of Lake George, ranging from the hundreds of pounds of pennies thrown in by modern tourists, back through the many years when the well stood open, to the 1750s, when a small number of musket balls, gunflints, and bits of pottery and glass were dropped into the very bottom (see the box "Beneath the Bubblegum"). Since we finished digging, the well still hasn't been filled in, but now there is a barrier at the top to keep tourists from throwing in modern artifacts.

The East Barracks (Site 4)

In the 1950s, Gifford believed that he had found and excavated substantial portions of the East Barracks at both the northeast and southeast corners of the parade ground. At its northern end he found the very deep remains of what he interpreted to be a blacksmith shop, containing many original tools (figs. 1.10 and 1.11). And at the south end he found five human skeletons inside what he believed was a casemate room; this may have been within the cellar of the East Barracks, and the skeletons were left on display until 1993 in what was popularly termed "the crypt."

In 1997 we dug into the northeast corner of the parade, probably very close to where Gifford had found his blacksmith shop. We found building rubble and black soil that was five to six feet thick, heavily disturbed but rich in artifacts (fig. 3.3). There were great numbers of bricks that appeared to be from a destroyed fireplace, alongside exploded pieces of mortar shells and the head from a felling ax. Below that depth we discovered burned timbers that were probably from the north end of the East Barracks, and these were concentrated at eight to nine feet down. The artifacts were interesting and even included a 1730 British halfpenny, but there was too much disturbance to allow us to interpret what had been constructed there, and modern artifacts were present even at depths of six feet or more. Because there was integrity at the very bottom of the pits, we wanted to see more, but unfortunately, the sand caved in so frequently that we were finally forced to give up. We did not return there after the first season.

We did further excavations in 1998 at a midpoint on the eastern side of the parade ground and were very excited to expose burned logs that were eight and one half feet deep; these were definitely from the western

★ Beneath the Bubblegum

Archaeologists in the 1950s were unable to reach the bottom of the garrison's stone-lined well, which was dug in 1756 by Rogers' Rangers, the famed company of rugged frontiersmen that fought against the French and Indians in the forests of New York and Canada. It was so deep and dangerous to explore that an effort to get to the bottom in 1958–1960 was called off. According to contemporary newspaper accounts, that first generation of archeologists, with only wood planking to brace the well stones against a cave-in, did reach Civil War levels before giving up.

When I began excavating within the fort in 1997, I knew I wouldn't be able to resist the lure of the well. My team and I purchased an electric hoist, built a massive cross-beam above the well, purchased sections of steel culvert with which to line the pit and a submersible pump for when we met water.

Starting down, I discovered that the top layer of debris was full of modern coins and artifacts. Since 1960 the well had been the center of attention for every schoolchild who visited the fort, and their excitement at seeing an open "wishing well" had left us with a forty-year legacy of tourist memorabilia. While modern material culture studies are popular in some quarters (most notably at the University of Arizona, which sponsors the famed Tucson Garbage Project), I was a neophyte at this sort of thing.

Wading in many feet of tourist rubbish, I sent up buckets of coins. The uppermost deposits contained great quantities of dimes, quarters, half-dollars, and even Susan B. Anthony dollars; children in the 1970s and 1960s were more frugal and had thrown in only pennies. Those who had no money or perhaps had better judgment had thrown in handfuls of crushed rock.

In this fashion, one handful at a time, I calculated that debris in the well—soda cans, sun-glasses, sheriff's badges, toy cars, flashbulbs and flash cubes, a small plastic skeleton, a black Batman action figure, and a tiny Creature from the Black Lagoon—had built up at the rate of about four inches a year. About nineteen feet down, I encountered hundreds of wads of chewing gum smack in the middle of what a garbologist would probably call the "flash-cube era." My students didn't mind rescuing Batman and the Creature from the well, but they never quite accepted my assertion that chewed-up gum has historical value.

I finally struck the water table at twenty-three feet, where contributions left by modern Americans ended. Here I found boards, no doubt used to shore up walls during the last attempt at excavation. Below this depth, I needed the pump. Many times it became clogged with sand and failed, or the circuit breaker flipped and cut off our power, leaving me standing in water up to my armpits, wondering when, or if, I would be hoisted to safety. But I was always in view; my assistant had installed a videocamera within the well shaft ten feet above me to record my every motion and word. This signal was broadcast to two monitors in the reconstructed barracks so that visitors could instantly see and hear everything I was doing below.

At twenty-five feet the nature of the fill changed; I was now working in fine sand and silt. I had gone deeper than the 1960 team had, and now I had groundwater rushing at me at a rate of about sixty gallons per minute. Crouched in the bottom of the thirty-six-inch-diameter well, wearing a safety harness and surrounded by my buckets, trowels, tape measures, and submersible pump, there was no room for error, no escape should anything go terribly wrong.

Then it happened. A cave-in. The first warning had been sand trickling down the sides of the

Lowering the culvert into the well at the start of the excavation.

Looking up the culvert from about twenty feet down inside the well. After this picture was taken, we had to dig down another ten feet.

Sunglasses discovered inside the well.

fallen well stones and went on to discover the complete skeleton of a goose, the end of a wooden barrel or keg, and even several pockets of pinecones and branches from the many years the well had stood open. More important, I learned how the soldiers had ingeniously managed to keep their well from filling in by lining the bottom with a watertight barrel to prevent the accumulation of silt. Massive and tightly joined, the barrel's vertical planks were waterlogged and swollen, and groundwater could flow into the well only by running over their tops or through knotholes.

Inside the barrel lining there were many small finds—a dozen lead musket balls; four French gunflints; a few dozen small pieces of lead (cut shot); fragments of pottery, porcelain, and window glass; the corner from a square-sided gin bottle; and even the bones of five frogs (see Appendix 2). Contrary to local lore, the well did not contain the fort's payroll, nor the bodies of female massacre victims. Instead, there was only a good representation of small, everyday objects from the 1750s. There were not the concentrated layers that would suggest that the well had been deliberately filled in or contaminated at the time of the massacre. At the very bottom, I exposed about twenty-seven inches of the barrel lining and reached a depth of nearly 30 feet. As I removed gravel and stones, sand bubbled up to take its place, and the entire thirty-foot-high well shaft, weighing many tons, sank nearly three feet into the quicksand. I finally signaled to be hoisted out, even as the shifting sand filled in the shaft around me.

Schoolchildren who visit Fort William Henry may find the soldiers' artifacts only slightly more interesting than those left by their counterparts thirty years ago, which are also on display. For them, flash cubes and outmoded Matchbox cars seem as remote as gunflints and musket balls.

culvert. This I had foolishly ignored. Suddenly, with a deafening roar, dozens of well stones came tumbling down through the narrow gap between the steel culvert and the lining of the well, hitting me from all sides, burying and silencing my pump. We had lowered the culvert by two feet only an hour earlier; otherwise, I unquestionably would have been killed by the avalanche of stones. As it was, I hopped forward and backward, attempting to avoid the falling rocks. My pump and electric hoist were dead, and the water was rising at an alarming rate. To make matters worse, my gyrations had thoroughly ensnared me in the safety harness, and I would have to make a Houdini-like escape.

Fortunately, my helpers at the top of the well were able to restore power to the hoist and they pulled me out, shaken but resolved to press on. In subsequent days I returned to remove the wall of the East Barracks. Initially, we were hopeful that we finally had a building outline that we could follow and use to define the entire row of buildings on the eastern side of the fort. Unfortunately, a massive cave-in buried one of our diggers up to his waist, and as the excavation grew larger, it became harder to route tourists around the pits. Here, too, we were forced to give up but not until after seeing enough to convince us that further work can unquestionably define the footprint of the East Barracks.

FIG. 3.3. Digging through layers of rubble at the north end of the East Barracks. Visitors would stare like this for hours.

The West Barracks (Sites 4, 8)

Before we began our excavations, we assumed that the reconstructed buildings of the fort had been placed *precisely* on top of their original foundations. We were not expecting to be able to dig into the ruins of any of the large barracks buildings simply because they had already been built upon. Consequently, we were caught by surprise when excavations in 1998 at the northwest corner of the parade ground (fig. 3.4) revealed a burned log wall running north-south. On the east side of the logs, the subsoil was absolutely sterile, whereas on the west side the soil was black and ashy. We could see that the surface was littered with sherds of white salt-glazed stoneware, porcelain, and even a British gunflint. We were looking over the top of a log wall at the interior of an eighteenth-century barracks, and it could only be the eastern side of the West Barracks.

FIG. 3.4. The excavation team trenching inside the ruins of the West Barracks in the summer of 1999. The reconstructed West Barracks is in the background.

FIG. 3.5. Log remains inside the West Barracks, facing south. The linear stain on the left is all that survives of the logs that made up the east wall of the barracks, while the string on the right marks the outline of a postmold. The base of the wood post is still intact.

This was a major discovery because fifteen feet away was the complete West Barracks as it had been rebuilt in the 1950s. And yet we had just found the foundation of the "real" West Barracks as it lies in the modern parade ground. The question we could not answer yet was whether the reconstruction was off by fifteen feet because they had not discovered where the foundation was, or had the builders made a very deliberate choice to *protect* the original fabric of the building? It gave us the opportunity to excavate inside the foundation from one of the largest buildings at the fort, so their decision not to build on the original foundation was the best choice they could possibly have made. We could only wonder whether the cellar might contain artifacts or bodies from the time of the siege or from the final moment when Indians entered the fort and killed the sick and injured.

We opened up huge trenches in 1999 and 2000 and exposed over fifty feet of the West Barracks wall, ever questioning whether we might descend into rooms containing charred remains from the fort's demise. We exposed about twenty feet of burned timbers in the bottom of one trench and found large post holes with the remains of posts alongside (fig. 3.5). The burned log wall became more intact the farther south we dug, and in spots we had as many as three charred logs still one on top of the other. In 1999, at a depth of about four feet below the modern surface of the parade, Matthew Rozell exposed a small room outlined with charred timbers, measuring just five by six feet (figs. 3.6 and 3.7). He also discovered piles of bricks from one of the barracks' fireplaces. In proceeding down into the cellar, we also found that the British fort was built on top of many prehistoric campsites and fishing stations, going back to at least the Early Archaic period. (See chap. 6.)

FIG. 3.6. Inside the remains of the West Barracks in the summer of 1999. Matthew Rozell (*left*) and John Farrell are examining the outline of a small room they have exposed. The first four feet below the parade ground was severely disturbed, and little soil layering was visible amid the pockets of brick, stone and ash.

FIG. 3.7. A closeup of the small room inside the West Barracks (fig. 3.6), facing west. Charred horizontal timbers define the room on the east and north. The scales are marked in 10-cm units.

The summer of 1999 ended with a massive cave-in of the whole trench, but when we resumed with our final field season in 2000, the crew made one of its very best discoveries, the imposing stone base of a barracks fireplace (fig. 3.8). Such a fireplace would have opened on both the north and south into rooms located on every floor of the barracks, thus heating several rooms at once. The surface of the fireplace base began between four and five feet below the current ground surface, and it extended down to a depth of about eight feet. (All of our measurements were taken in the metric system, so we measured down 1.28 m to the top of the fireplace and more than 2 m to the very bottom.) The stones were massive and mortared together, with the entire feature measuring nine feet on a side; part of the fireplace had been cut away during the West Barracks reconstruction in the 1950s, so we now knew that the builders *had* encountered the original barracks foundation and chose not to build on it.

FIG. 3.8. The side of a massive stone fireplace base inside the West Barracks, facing southwest. Although the stone base is quite intact here at the eight-foot depth, its upper levels were largely removed during the 1950s reconstruction of the barracks.

As we worked our way down to the bottom, inside the cellar of the barracks, we discovered a rich matrix of bricks, mortar, scattered fireplace stones, and nails, and then we hit a charcoal lens two inches (5 cm) thick at a depth of 75 inches (1.9 m). This was all that was left of the floorboards from the first floor of the barracks, and it appears these boards had dropped down into the cellar during the final conflagration. Then, from 75 to 79 inches (1.9 to 2.0 m), we discovered a layer of dark earth (without charcoal) that contained many period artifacts: at least thirteen gunflints, a frog (scabbard holder), many sherds of white, salt-glazed stoneware (some with Scratch Blue decoration), part of a wine bottle, and many animal bones, all found very close to the base of the fireplace and resting just above what had been the floor of the cellar. Also, on the bottom floor we discovered several dozen mouse skulls; perhaps they had enjoyed the fort's food supply, but since they were not charred, it is also possible that the mice had moved in and created nests after the abandonment of the fort. Below this, at 79 inches (2.0 m), the earth became hard-packed, perhaps representing the actual floor that soldiers walked upon. And below that, there was nothing but fine beach sand, no doubt predating the arrival of the army; we cored down to 102 inches (2.6 m) to make sure, but it was quite sterile.

This stratigraphic layering is clearly critical to the interpretation of the building in that it demonstrates how the barracks burned and collapsed into the cellar below. We found no traces of massacre victims on the bottom floor, although that is still a possibility if the rest of the cellar were to be excavated. In measuring the placement of the fireplace base relative to the burned logs of the eastern barracks wall, we determined that the walkway on either side of the fireplace was about five feet wide. So with a fireplace width of nine feet and the open floor measuring about five feet on either side, the total width of the East Barracks was roughly nineteen to twenty feet. As we concluded our work on the fireplace, we left everything as we found it and then backfilled the cellar (fig. 3.9).

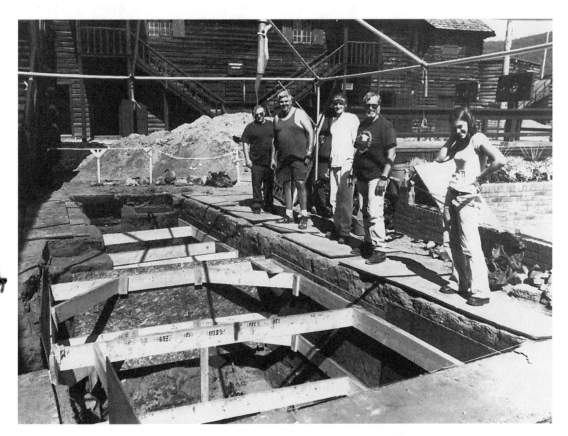

FIG. 3.9. The team that finished excavating the West Barracks in 2000. Sheets of plywood and 2-x-8s were required to brace every wall against the possibility of cave-ins. John Kosek, the group's supervisor, is second from the left.

However, we did take several samples of burned logs from the barracks wall and wrapped the wood in airtight plastic so that we can later identify the species of wood.

Ironically, and sadly, the excavation of the fireplace and cellar generated so much excitement among visitors to the fort that we watched an eight-year-old boy literally fall and break his arm as he tried to run closer to the excavation. It is rather humbling to realize that archeology can have such an effect upon the public, but the very act of discovery *is* a powerful draw.

The artifacts found elsewhere inside the West Barracks foundation (see Appendix 2 for an enumeration, and for illustrations see chap. 5, as noted below) included buttons, buckles, cuff links, a finger ring (fig. 5.16), a broken bayonet (fig. 5.14), the stem from a wineglass (fig. 5.10, *top left*), a beautiful delft medicine cup (fig. 5.7), gaming pieces of lead, the corner of a grinding stone, the base from a case bottle, the delicate bone inlay from the handle of a knife (fig. 5.16, *top right*), a pair of scissors, a tiny brass spoon (fig. 5.5), at least two fishhooks, and thousands of burned fragments of animal bones. And all through the foundation we found exploded pieces of mortar shells and canister shot, as well as musket balls and gunflints. While many of the pieces of mortar shells may be French, lobbed over the walls into the fort, some were no doubt British shells that had blown apart prematurely.

We found sewing supplies in the ruins of the barracks, including a thimble, a needle, and eighteen straight pins. This provides tantalizing evidence for at least a modicum of normalcy at this frontier site. Ceramics include sherds of delft; slip-decorated, buff-bodied earthenware; white and gray salt-glazed stoneware; porcelain; and redware, along with lots of tobacco pipes. We also found two regimental buttons from the Revolutionary War: a British Twenty-second Regiment button and a First Battalion Pennsylvania button (fig. 5.18). These buttons may suggest that later armies camped atop (or at least passed by) the burned ruins of the old fort, but we also know that soldiers were housed nearby in hospitals during the Revolution. Either way, the story of Fort William Henry would have been well known to all, and curious soldiers during the next war probably loved poking into the charred ruins.

Archeology outside the Reconstructed Fort

The Parking Lot Area (Sites 1, 7, 10)

Efforts to find intact dumps or outworks on the west side of the fort, around the edges of the modern parking lot, were largely unsuccessful.

In 1997 Susan Winchell-Sweeney directed a team in the cemetery area (Site 1), where she discovered several of Gifford's old excavation trenches, perhaps the very ones he used to find the cemetery in 1953. Still, there were few artifacts and far too much disturbance. An excavation conducted in 1998 underneath the parking lot just east of the Trolley Restaurant on Canada Street (Site 7) encountered even fewer artifacts. And in 1999 an effort to find a breastworks just west of the fort (Site 10) recovered many nineteenth- and twentieth-century artifacts but little from the period of the fort. All of these areas appeared to have potential, but they best reflect the 240+ years of activities that postdate the destruction of the fort.

The Moat (Site 9)

In 1999 we dug inside the moat, or ditch, on the western side of the fort (just north of the modern entrance into the fort). In deposits consisting of coarse sandy fill, we found three-inch-thick planks from a wood platform or walkway of early-twentieth-century origin; a modern roofing nail and fragments of beer bottles were found underneath the platform. Given its placement, this may have been used by tourists visiting from the Fort William Henry Hotel and walking through the ruins. Unfortunately, while the small artifact sample included five musket balls, there was no clear soil layering, and everything appeared to be disturbed.

The Lawn South of the Tower Theater Building (Site 13)

In the summer of 2000 we placed several pits in the open lawn south of the Tower Theater building, hoping to find evidence of the French bombardment. This location is several hundred feet northwest of the reconstructed fort and may be fairly close to the site of the French siege trenches. However, although we found a cluster of pig bones, a musket ball, a few sherds, and some prehistoric flakes of quartz and chert, there were no cultural features, so the testing was ended after a week.

The Dump East of the Fort (Site 5)

Historical records suggest that the soldiers at Fort William Henry were often dirty and suffered from poor sanitary conditions; and with perhaps five hundred people packed into a relatively small area, they no doubt generated a considerable amount of garbage over the two years they lived in the fort. We were not sure where dumping had occurred, but we noticed that the reconstructed fort had been built very close to the edge of the old lake terrace that it sits on, with a steep downhill slope on the east. We knew that most dumping at military sites typically occurs on slopes, even as level land is reserved for buildings. We decided to investigate.

A team led by Andrew Farry began to trench outside the east wall of the fort in 1997, and within just a few days they discovered an unbelievably rich trash deposit, what must have been the main dump for the entire fort. They also began finding burned timbers from the fort, and all of this commenced about four to five feet down. As work continued in 1998, a burned layer was found under six feet of mixed soil deposit; it probably represented the burning of the fort in 1757.

Excavations into the dump continued for three years, culminating in 1999 with the construction of a huge "step trench" running up the side

FIG. 3.10. A scene reminiscent of a nineteenth-century dig through a mound or tell. The dump east of the fort was so deep that it became necessary to dig a step trench up the slope; "stepping down" the sides of the trench helped to protect the diggers from a cave-in. If the trench walls had been dug vertically, down to a depth of eleven or twelve feet, then lives could have been lost if the cross-bracing gave way.

of the slope (fig. 3.10). As the trench approached the wall of the fort, cultural deposits became deeper, and diggers at the bottom of the trench were unearthing artifacts at eleven and twelve feet below the modern surface. Massive cross-bracing of the sandy walls of the trench was required, but it was worth the effort. Virtually all types of garbage were buried here, with food remains predominating; there were nearly 16,000 fragments of butchered bones, especially cow, pig, and fish bones. There were some 75 musket balls, 35 whole or broken British gunflints, 32 whole or broken French gunflints, 35 badly preserved metal buttons, 3 sets of cuff links, 5 buckles, 2 British halfpennies, 1 Spanish silver real, two Jew's Harps, many hundreds of pottery sherds, and hundreds of fragments of wine bottles (see Appendix 2).

Because all of this was within just a few feet of the outer wall of the fort, it strongly suggests that the soldiers went the shortest possible distance to dispose of their trash. The statement made by Lieutenant-Colonel Ralph Burton in his 1756 letter definitely comes to mind: "The fort stinks enough to cause an infection." Archeological evidence is essentially in agreement; given the proximity of the dump to the wall of the fort, Fort William Henry probably stank in the summertime!

One feature we failed to discover outside the eastern wall of the fort was the roadbed of the original military road that ran up to the entrance of the fort. In 1998 we excavated a lengthy trench up the side of the slope (fig. 3.11), but we found no evidence of a hard-packed surface that would suggest a former road.

Future Work

At the end of every excavation, someone always asks whether there is anything left that we would still like to unearth. At Fort William Henry the answer is the same as when we started, a resounding yes! For starters, I would still like to see much more work done within the foundations of both the East and West Barracks; we need better definition of their limits and a determination of whether traces of massacre victims lie inside. Also, we did no excavations underneath any of the reconstructed buildings of the fort, and I would especially like to see pits dug under the North Barracks. (This reconstruction has no cellar under it, so we hope that nothing has been disturbed.) Even the well can use some additional digging because we never exposed all of the barrel lining at the bottom; this could be accomplished by installing well points all around the shaft and preventing ground water from seeping in while the excavation is being completed.

Finally and most important, much more testing should be done to

FIG. 3.11. A long trench was dug across the base of the slope east of the fort in the search for evidence of the original road that led into the fort. Lake George is just out of sight in the background, behind the former Delaware and Hudson Railroad station and cruise boats.

locate all of the fort's cemetery. Until that happens, there may well be hundreds of skeletons that will eventually be disturbed by utility lines or new construction. Ideally, archeological testing should be done underneath the modern parking lot in as many places as possible.

Still, so much archeology has already been done at Fort William Henry that it will not hurt to "save some" for the future. Forty years went by between Stanley Gifford's work and our own, and I feel it is important that we allow the fort to retain some of its mystique by *not* digging everything up. Then, once another forty years has passed, the next generation of archeologists will probably experience as much excitement as we did. And I want to be there to watch them!

Chapter 4

The Men and Women
Who Died at the Fort

Background

LIFE WAS EXCEPTIONALLY GRIM throughout the two years that soldiers garrisoned Fort William Henry, and this is best judged by the large number of soldiers who died from disease, injuries, and Indian raids. Smallpox was especially severe, and while there is no exact count of how many succumbed, estimates have ranged from several hundred up to a thousand. Because of illness, the real strength of the garrison was often far less than the number of soldiers would imply, and it is often stated that on military campaigns far more men died from disease than from battle. This was certainly true at Fort William Henry, and it is ironic that more men probably died from disease than from the infamous siege and massacre.

Contemporary and later historical sources have calculated that as many as two hundred to three hundred casualties occurred during the course of the siege, although historian Ian Steele, in his book *Betrayals*, has argued for a lower figure. Subsequently, in what is usually described as the first stage of the massacre, many of the seventy or so sick and wounded soldiers lying inside casemate rooms under the ramparts were killed by Indians on August 9. As the French looked on, Indians entered the fort and scalped those who had been too weak to leave with the army. The number of those killed at that time has been variously estimated; for example, Dr. Miles Whitworth, a surgeon who had attended the soldiers, later stated that the number killed and scalped inside the fort was about eighty-seven. Père Pierre Roubaud observed one of the Indians leaving the fort with a grisly trophy, a human head still dripping blood. Roubaud, while there to minister to the Christian Abenakis, was later instrumental in helping to redeem captives from the Indians.

On the following day, August 10, another seventeen wounded British soldiers were taken from their huts within the entrenched camp and killed and scalped by Indians, while their French guards did nothing to protect them. Later that day, as the column of soldiers and dependents marched down the military road toward Fort Edward, another 185 British and Americans—perhaps more—were killed during the final stage of the massacre. Their bodies were left strewn along the road, where clusters of them were observed in the days that followed.

Procuring scalps and prisoners were the primary motivations for what had transpired, but some of the Indians also dug up part of the fort's cemetery on August 9. They scalped the corpses of soldiers who most likely had died from smallpox, removing their red coats and blankets as booty. Richard Rogers, a brother of the Ranger leader Robert Rogers, was one of those abused in this way. John Cuneo has described this contemptible act and its aftermath:

> The reports from the Lake George front bore particularly sad news to Robert. Richard, the one brother who seems to have been closest to him, had died of smallpox on 22 June—"no small loss to us," wrote Major

FIG. 4.1. Excavation in the military cemetery in the 1950s. Each rectangular outline represents a grave shaft. Fort William Henry Museum.

General Webb. Later Robert heard that he was one of the corpses dug up to be scalped by the maddened Indians after the fort's surrender. But the dead had their revenge—a smallpox epidemic broke out among their desecrators, who carried it back to spread death among distant tribes on the Mississippi.

Native people were just as susceptible to smallpox as were Europeans, if not more so, and diseased bodies were discovered along trails on the route to Canada. Some tribes, such as the Potawatomi, were decimated by smallpox, and it can easily be said that the spread of the epidemic may have been the most remarkable outcome of the siege at Fort William Henry.

Twenty years later, during the American Revolution, smallpox hospitals were constructed close to the ruins of Fort William Henry, and it is possible that many more bodies were buried nearby at that time. When considering these and the earlier deaths, it is clear that well over a thousand soldiers or dependents were buried either around or within the ruins of the fort; others would have been buried in the vicinity of the entrenched camp and still more along the military road. Some of these would have been individual graves; others may have been mass graves. It must be recognized, however, that those at the entrenched camp or at the massacre site may have received no burial at all before animals tore their bodies apart. Presumably, French and Indian casualties were buried elsewhere within the village of Lake George, but their locations are unknown.

Human Remains Discovered during the 1950s Excavation

No maps have survived to show where soldiers were buried, although twentieth-century construction within the community of Lake George often revealed human remains. When the excavations commenced at Fort William Henry in the 1950s, Stanley Gifford made it a priority to locate the military cemetery, and he trenched south of the fort until the dark stains representing grave shafts began to appear. The public response to the discovery was phenomenal, and the owners of Fort William Henry decided that the skeletons would become part of the permanent exhibits of the fort. Ten burials were pedestaled and excavated within the cemetery (figs. 4.1 and 4.2), while other skeletons were found more randomly throughout the ruins of the fort (figs. 4.3 and 4.4). The individuals in the cemetery were excavated throughout the winter of 1953–1954, at which time they were kept surrounded with heating cables provided by General Electric; this was done so that the bones would not be damaged by freezing. A permanent log structure was built around the skeletons to protect them while they were being viewed, and the bones remained on display until 1993.

Of the human remains discovered inside the fort, the most gruesome discovery was a cluster of five intermingled skeletons, found in 1957 underneath a brick floor at the south end of the East Barracks. One of them had eight musket balls scattered within its bones, one was missing its skull, and many of the bones showed signs of trauma. Gifford immediately concluded that these five individuals were among those killed on August 9, and their presence underneath a brick floor at least suggested that they had received an impromptu burial after their deaths. This was a spectacular discovery, and the bones were arranged as an exhibit within what the fort's staff termed "the crypt" (fig. 4.5).

Both the skeletons in the crypt and those in the cemetery became immensely popular attractions for visitors, and bones became a significant part of the advertising at the reconstructed fort (fig. 4.6). However,

FIG. 4.2. Excavation in the military cemetery in the 1950s. The wooden stakes were being used to test for the presence of bones. Fort William Henry Museum.

FIG. 4.3. A human skull discovered during the excavation of Fort William Henry in the 1950s. Fort William Henry Museum.

another very popular exhibit was the unusually well-preserved human scalp that had been found in 1954 stuck to the side of a mortar shell (fig. 4.7). This was the only scalp ever unearthed at the fort, but unfortunately it was burned and lost when the reconstructed West Barracks was destroyed by fire in 1967.

Modern Analysis

While the popularity of Fort William Henry's skeletons showed no signs of fading, museums across the United States began to adopt new policies toward the display of human remains. For this reason, it was finally decided to remove the fort's bones from view. In early 1993 two forensic anthropologists, Maria Liston and Brenda Baker, carefully removed the years of dirt from the bones, mapped the remains in situ, and reassem-

FIG. 4.4. A human skeleton discovered in the ruins of Fort William Henry in the 1950s. Fort William Henry Museum.

FIG. 4.5. The five victims of the massacre who were discovered in a casemate or cellar room in 1957. Fort William Henry Museum.

FIG. 4.6. A humorous advertising pose from the 1950s. Betty Campbell of the Betty Campbell Model Agency is holding one of the skulls unearthed by Stanley Gifford. "Alas poor Hawk-eye, I knew him well!" Fort William Henry Museum.

disrespectful

FIG. 4.7. An intact English mortar shell with some black human hair and a scalp attached to it. This was discovered inside the ruins of one of the barracks buildings. Fort William Henry Museum.

bled the skeletons that had become disarticulated over the years (figs. 4.8 and 4.9). They then painstakingly removed the bones from the ground and began the lengthy process of analysis to determine the age, sex, probable race, general health, and cause of death of each individual; they also began the search for evidence of trauma, disease, and stress. These studies are ongoing and are revealing the many types of hardships undergone by eighteenth-century soldiers who were far from home. So far, Liston and Baker have found evidence for herniated disks, severe arthritis, abscessed teeth, systemic infection, and more. Smallpox, as a

FIG. 4.8. Dr. Maria Liston and volunteers mapping human skeletons inside the military cemetery in 1993.

relatively quick killer, does not leave clear evidence on bone, so it cannot be revealed by their study.

The five individuals discovered in the crypt have been the most enlightening because they represent the soldiers who were most likely to have been killed at the time of the massacre. Liston and Baker summarized their findings in the *International Journal of Osteoarchaeology*:

> Four of the five men sustained pre-mortem leg trauma that would have resulted in their hospitalization and prevented them from walking. The other massive perimortem trauma on these remains vividly depicts the results of the massacre. Three of the five men were shot in the knee; two of these three were shot elsewhere as well. One man was decapitated. Both the front and back of the bodies bear cut marks, probably from the use of both axes and long-bladed knives as weapons. The numerous gashes in the thoracic and pelvic regions indicate the men were mutilated.

The evidence for mutilation is especially disturbing, but forensic anthropologists like to say that "bones don't lie." The final moments of life for these unfortunate victims must have been terrifying, yet they are finally able to tell their story to modern scholars (see the box "Bones Tell the Story.")

The individual who was beheaded may very well have been the one whose head was described by Père Pierre Roubaud. His second cervical vertebra has four cut marks on it, whereas the top of the process was cut clean through. The bones of this same individual were covered with a pattern of wounds that suggest he was cut with at least two different

FIG. 4.9. One of the soldiers' skeletons in the military cemetery, lying on top of what appears to be a slab of pine bark. This extended skeleton was unearthed by Gifford in the 1950s, but with the passage of time it had become absolutely black with dirt and spiders.

★ Bones Tell the Story

The work done by Maria Liston and Brenda Baker on the bones at Fort William Henry is part of a rapidly-growing field known as forensic anthropology. These biological anthropologists typically use bones to determine the causes of death of modern murder victims; and some scientists, such as Clyde C. Snow, a freelance consultant, and the late William Maples at the C. A. Pound Human Identification Laboratory, have achieved formidable reputations by studying the remains of modern massacre victims in Bosnia, Argentina, and elsewhere, as well as the bodies of celebrities such as Dr. Josef Mengele and the czar's family in Russia. Similar studies have been done on the bones of Native Americans dating back thousands of years and on skeletons in colonial cemeteries that have had to be moved due to modern construction.

However, surprisingly few early soldiers' bones have been studied, other than those at Snake Hill, a War of 1812 cemetery in Fort Erie, Ontario, and the few skeletons discovered in the 1980s at the 1876 site of the Little Bighorn in Montana. The skeletons unearthed at Fort William Henry thus represent the first eighteenth-century soldiers in the United States to receive this type of analysis, and they provide a rare opportunity to determine how severe life was for men who were expected to perform rigorous manual labor while receiving little medical attention.

Some mortuary scientists specialize on soft tissue analysis, but forensic anthropologists focus on bones and all of the stories they have to tell. To determine the gender of an individual, they rely most heavily upon pelvic characteristics, the chin, the brow ridges over the eyes, the size of the mastoid process behind the ear, and the overall robustness of the skeleton, especially in the areas of muscle attachment. Age is best deter- mined by examining the eruption sequence of the teeth, the degree to which the sutures of the skull have fused, and the degree to which the epiphyses have fused onto the ends of the long bones, indicating that an individual has reached maturity and has stopped growing. Racial characteristics are established by measuring the breadth of the face, the shape of the nasal aperture, the appearance of the chin, and the overall shape of the skull. None of these criteria is ever infallible; for example, the skeleton from a robust, physically active woman may easily be misinterpreted for that of a man if only part of the bones are present. Only by examining multiple characteristics in combination, preferably from a large population, is there a reasonable chance of accuracy.

Perhaps the most significant aspect of the bones at Fort William Henry is their ability to reveal a variety of diseases and nutritional problems that can leave distinct traces on bone. Tuberculosis, for example, leaves tiny holes or "pitting" on the bones, and tuberculosis of the spine causes the vertebral bodies to collapse into each other. Syphilis and anemia also leave pitting on the skull, whereas cavities, caries and various types of periodontal disease may leave gaping holes in the teeth and jaws. Tumors show a thickening of bone and bone spurs, whereas arthritis results in an "eating away" of the ends of the long bones. The significance of the bones at Fort William Henry certainly lies in their ability to show all of these conditions among the soldiers, thus confirming historical sources that suggest much sickness at the fort.

The evidence for trauma and injury is equally rich, including scalping marks along the front edge of at least one skull and a variety of knife marks on bones of the chest and abdomen; one individual had a musket ball embedded at the distal end of his left humerus, and the patellas, or kneecaps, of several individuals in the crypt had been destroyed by musket fire. Evidence for medical procedures is also good at Fort William Henry, including amputated limbs with no signs of bone regrowth, suggesting that the patient did not recover. Rarely has a collection of human bones revealed so much information about the lives and deaths of early Americans. Since this is a very small sample of those who died at the fort, undoubtedly much more may be learned if the rest of the military cemetery is ever investigated.

weapons, both from the front and from behind, and his pubic area was cut in such a way as to suggest genital mutilation as well. In fact, all five of the men in the crypt demonstrated genital mutilation, and the patterns of cut marks in their stomach and chest areas suggest they were disemboweled too.

Although the results provided by Liston and Baker have been stunning, their task has not been easy. All of the skeletons have been difficult to analyze because the bones had been covered repeatedly with alvar (liquid plastic preservative), glue, varnish, and other adhesives since their original discovery, apparently in a misguided effort to preserve them. Also, the bones of many of the skeletons had been moved from body to body, thoroughly mixing them up, and some had even been splattered with red paint. Physical anthropologists do not need help like this.

Because some of the skeletons had been so altered since 1954, Liston and Baker sorely needed more intact remains to study. Fortunately, this came in 1995 when they were able to return to the cemetery for the filming of the show *The New Detectives* on the Discovery Channel. At that time they uncovered an additional eight grave shafts and excavated three of them. Until that time, all of the skeletons they had examined were Caucasian, or white; bone measurements indicated they were chiefly men, although there was evidence for women and at least one child. The 1995 work was especially significant because one of the skeletons discovered was that of an African American. Also, they found a number of artifacts together with the bodies, including soldiers' buttons, and so they are better able to study the soldiers' burial customs.

The 1997–2000 Project

When I began my own project at Fort William Henry in 1997, I did not feel that was necessary to expose more of the soldiers' skeletons, although I knew it was possible that we might accidentally stumble across some. After all, the research by Liston and Baker is still continuing on the thirty to forty previously discovered skeletons; and until that work is finished, it really is not ethical to uncover more. Still, I believe that it is important to discover where hundreds of other soldiers' skeletons still lie so that they can be protected and honored. Stanley Gifford did some archeological testing underneath the parking lot of the reconstructed fort, and in doing so *did* discover additional human bones. When the surface of the parking lot is eventually repaved, I feel it is important to do new testing at that time.

Even though we deliberately avoided looking for human bones between 1997 and 2000 and found none, this did not stop visitors from asking us daily whether we had found any. It is curious that even today, when it is no longer considered respectful to unearth human remains, the public absolutely demands to see skeletons. Some actually became aggressive and were positively incensed because we had none to show. I do not pretend to understand this fascination with the dead, but every archeologist has witnessed it firsthand. It seems that everyone wants to watch someone else's ancestors dug up, but not their own.

Chapter 5

The Artifacts They Left Behind

Artifacts Unearthed in the 1950s

A RTIFACTS ARE THE MAINSTAY of the archeologist, and they help us to tell stories that are rather different from those of historians. People often tell me excitedly how much they enjoy visiting archeological sites, yet "how boring" they find history in general. Part of the difference seems to be that they enjoy watching objects come out of the ground, and they are thrilled when given the chance to hold artifacts in their hands. The average person can experience a very tangible link with the people of the past when he or she can actually see and touch something that is old. It is a personal bond of sorts between the artifact's user of two hundred years ago and the modern visitor to a historic site who merely asks that his experience be "relevant" and entertaining for a few hours.

Part of what makes Fort William Henry so appealing, then, must be that the scale of the 1950s excavations was enormous, and tens of thousands of artifacts were recovered from the parade ground, from inside the foundations of the barracks buildings, and especially from inside the ruins of the northwest bastion. Stanley Gifford reported on these extensively to the newspapers and did some cataloging of the artifacts that went on display or into storage. However, while many artifacts have been numbered and listed on file cards, there is no master catalog that lists everything that was found and identifies precisely *where* artifacts were found. Provenance information is everything to the archeologist, and we cannot do much interpretation if we don't know what layer the object came from or which foundation or what was lying next to it in the ground. Trying to understand a past excavation without all of the records is rather like trying to communicate with treasure hunters—most of the information has been lost, so there isn't much of a story left.

Having expressed these cautions, it nevertheless is possible to survey the huge 1950s collections at Fort William Henry and get a general sense of what was used and consumed at this frontier fort. The storage boxes that house Gifford's finds contain thousands of wrought-iron nails, spikes, tobacco pipes (fig. 5.1), wine bottle fragments, musket balls, and buckshot (fig. 5.2); as well as hundreds of gunflints, mortar shell fragments (fig. 5.3), and plain metal buttons; dozens of ax heads, knives, bayonet fragments, buckles, and musket parts (fig. 5.4); and smaller numbers of "shod" spades, hoes, cannonballs, tin canteen fragments, and pewter spoon fragments. There also are large charcoalized beams and masses of charcoal in the storage collection. Curiously, the collection includes very few butchered animal bones, making it difficult to say much about the soldiers' diet, and there are very few pottery sherds from the period. There are a few sherds on exhibit, but all are from nineteenth- and twentieth-century vessels. Newspaper accounts of the 1950s also describe how Gifford found such distinctive artifacts as a 1531 Spanish coin, a cache of over fifty grapeshot, and a half-moon-shaped metal gorget.

The exhibits in the reconstructed West and North Barracks at Fort William Henry display some of the better examples of these artifacts; the fort also displays artifacts from the bottom of Lake George and

FIG. 5.1. Some of the tobacco pipe stems and bowls discovered at Fort William Henry in the 1950s.

FIG. 5.2. Some of the lead buckshot discovered at Fort William Henry in the 1950s.

FIG. 5.3. Examples of mortar shell fragments discovered at Fort William Henry in the 1950s.

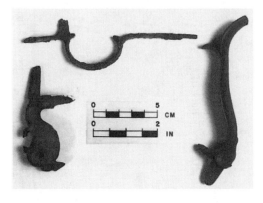

FIG. 5.4. Some of the musket parts discovered at Fort William Henry in the 1950s: a trigger guard, a gun cock, and a butt plate.

other material donated to the fort by local residents. Storage space is limited at present, but The Fort William Henry Corporation has plans to develop a suitable long-term curation facility, where it will be easier to study these collections.

Artifacts Found during the 1990s Excavations

While our diggers were working inside and outside the reconstructed walls of Fort William Henry, we always had a laboratory crew laboring inside one of the barracks, performing the necessary tasks of washing, sorting, labeling, and identifying the artifacts just as soon as possible after they came out of the field. Their leader was Merle Parsons, a retired social studies teacher who enjoyed having "older" students to instruct. During our first field season in 1997, our lab crew was based in the exhibit room at the south end of the parade ground, where visitors would file by, constantly asking questions about everything that had been found. The problem was that only a flimsy rope barrier separated them from us, and we couldn't get much work done. This room was then

Table 5.1

Artifacts Recovered from Fort William Henry, 1997–2000

CERAMIC SHERDS

Redware	Delft	Buff-bodied slipware	White salt-glazed stoneware	Gray salt-glazed stoneware	Brown salt-glazed stoneware	Unrefined stoneware	Porcelain
261	359	15	424	184	2	89	366
(15.4%)	(21.1%)	(0.9%)	(24.9%)	(10.8%)	—	(5.2%)	(21.5%)

GLASS (HOLLOWWARE) FRAGMENTS

Wine bottle	Case bottle	Tableware	Vial/medicine bottle
1,004	212	279	128

ARMAMENTS

Musket balls	Cut lead shot	Grapeshot	Canister shot	Mortar shell fragments	Worms	Gunflints (British)	Gunflints (French)	Gunflints (burned)[a]	Bayonet fragments	Musket parts	Gun furniture
251	14	13	18	18	3	76	88	17	2	1	2

PERSONAL ADORNMENT

Buttons[b] (metal)	Buttons (wood)	Buttons (bone)	Buttons (regimental)	Cuff links	Rings	Buckles
88	3	1	3	8	1	24

ANIMAL BONE AND TOOTH FRAGMENTS

27,937

OTHER

Cast-iron pot/kettle	Fishhooks	Knives	Forks	Spoons	Scissors	Pins	Needles	Thimbles	Mouth harps	British halfpennies	Spanish reals
3	4	6	2	5	2	25	1	1	2	6	2

[a] The burned gunflints cannot be identified as to color.   [b] Most of the buttons are so fragmentary that no designs can be identified.

turned into archeology exhibit space, and for the next three years, Merle's team shifted to one of the ground-floor rooms in the North Barracks. In their new space, visitors were allowed only to peer in through the open door; that gave them more privacy, except for the occasional tourist who stared in as if to say, "How dare you keep us out!"

Before we began our project, we undeniably were impressed by the bushels of artifacts that Stanley Gifford had found in the 1950s, and so we may have assumed that we would be satiated with a daily fare of cannonballs, mortar shells, swords, and human skeletons. Unfortunately, that was not the case, but we did find a wonderful variety of the very ordinary things that soldiers, officers, and camp followers had left behind. Many of the artifacts that we excavated over the past four years are still being analyzed, but some totals are presented here (table 5.1), and more detailed listings are given, site by site, in Appendix 2.

The most common artifacts in all of our pits were certainly the thousands of wrought-iron nails and brick fragments, especially inside the cellars of the West and East Barracks. However, architectural evidence was really rather limited: we found very few hinges, only one door handle (at the north end of the parade), no door latches, and a single lock plate (the Site 5 dump). Tools of any type were also in short supply because we found only one ax in the East Barracks at the north end of the parade and one ax in the well, plus a few knife, fork, and spoon fragments (fig. 5.5) and fishhooks. These were chiefly found in the Site 5 dump and inside the West Barracks.

Evidence for food and foodways was far better represented, both through the ceramic vessels that were used for serving or storage and the many thousands of butchered bones that were found inside the West

FIG. 5.5. A small brass spoon fragment discovered inside the West Barracks.

FIG. 5.6. Examples of ceramic sherds found at Fort William Henry: *Top:* buff-bodied, slip-decorated earthenware and delft; *bottom:* white, salt-glazed stoneware with "Scratch Blue" decoration.

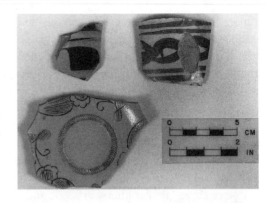

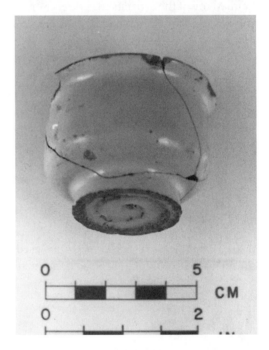

FIG. 5.7. A small medicine cup of delft, discovered inside the West Barracks.

Barracks and in the dump east of the fort. Sherds from plates, bowls, and cups of white, salt-glazed stoneware, delft and porcelain accounted for over 67 percent of the ceramic assemblage (figs. 5.6 and 5.7), and there were only three fragments of cast-iron pots or kettles, which would have been used for cooking. A great many of the bone fragments were small and burned, but studies of the bones now being conducted by Jene Romeo of Hunter College, CUNY, suggest that beef and pork predominated in the meat portion of the diet, along with a lesser amount of mutton and fish. Perhaps the strangest context in which we found bones was the well, which contained thirty-nine bones from a single goose (fig. 5.8) and eight pelves from five different frogs. The goose had clearly not been eaten, but we are not sure whether it dated to the occupation of the fort or whether it had fallen in slightly later.

Glass was present in sizable quantities, consisting chiefly of wine bottles, along with smaller quantities of straight-sided "case" bottles, medicine vials, and tableware (figs. 5.9 and 5.10). Both the wine bottles and the tableware predominated in the Site 5 dump, the West Barracks, and

FIG. 5.8. Some of the bones from a goose discovered inside the well.

FIG. 5.9. Fragments of case bottles and (*far right*) a base from a medicine bottle discovered at Fort William Henry.

FIG. 5.10. Fragments of tablewares (*top row*) and the base from a medicine bottle (*bottom*) discovered at Fort William Henry.

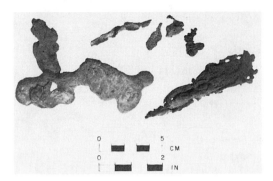

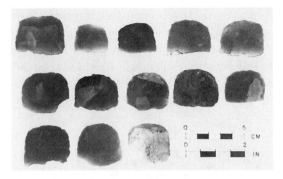

FIG. 5.11. Examples of lead sprue discovered at Fort William Henry.

FIG. 5.12. Examples of gunflints discovered in the Site 5 dump.

near the cemetery, whereas case bottles were most common in the Site 5 dump. The medicine vials were not clustered in a specific location, so we cannot say where a makeshift hospital may have been, but they did appear to be most common at the north end of the parade and in the West Barracks. No tabulation was done of fragments of window glass, most of which appeared to be of quite recent origin.

Armaments were well represented throughout many of our sites, with musket balls and gunflints predominating. Some 251 musket balls were recovered, ranging in diameter from 57 to 69 caliber, and they were especially common in the West Barracks and the Site 5 dump. The most pieces of lead slag, the residue from casting musket balls in molds, were discovered at the north end of the parade ground, suggesting that this was one of the places where soldiers occupied themselves in their spare time (fig. 5.11). Gunflints and gun spalls were almost evenly divided between those of British and French origin (fig. 5.12), although the French ones were slightly more numerous (88 vs. 76). Mortar shell fragments were most common in the West Barracks and at the north end of the parade ground, presumably where the most French shells were landing during the siege. It was disappointing, but not surprising, that there were very few musket parts or gun furniture (fig. 5.13), and only a single bayonet was discovered inside the West Barracks (fig. 5.14). However, these artifact types would have been highly prized and are invariably rare on military sites.

The most interesting artifacts on every historical site tend to be those that are more personalized, which give some sense of the user who lost or broke a button, for example. Consequently, buttons, cuff links, buckles, and finger rings are always welcome finds. A total of eight sets of cuff links were found, from the West Barracks, the south end of the parade ground, and from the Site 5 dump (fig. 5.15). A single undecorated

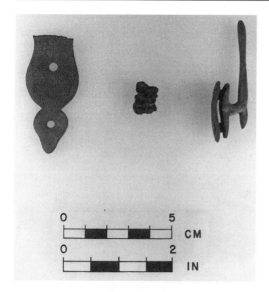

FIG. 5.13. An escutcheon, a worm, and a brass scabbard holder discovered at Fort William Henry.

FIG. 5.14. A bayonet, with tip missing, discovered in the cellar of the West Barracks.

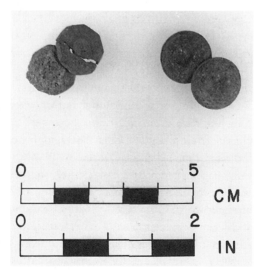

FIG. 5.15. Examples of cuff links from the south end of the parade ground (*left*) and the Site 5 dump (*right*).

FIG. 5.16. A brass thimble, the bone inlay from a knife handle, and a plain finger ring, all discovered inside the cellar of the West Barracks.

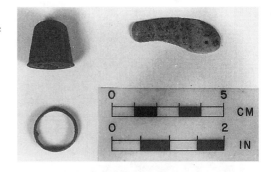

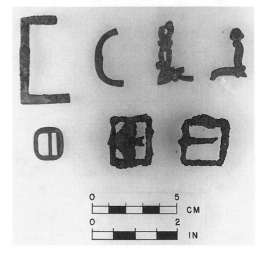

FIG. 5.17. Examples of buckles discovered at Fort William Henry.

finger ring was found inside the cellar of the West Barracks (fig. 5.16). Buckles were slightly more common, including shoe buckles of brass or copper alloy and utilitarian or harness buckles of iron. These were found in the West Barracks, the Site 5 dump, at the north end of the parade ground, and at the edge of the military cemetery (fig. 5.17).

The vast majority of the buttons unearthed at Fort William Henry were undecorated, and many were extremely corroded and fragmentary. Interestingly, three regimental buttons were discovered that were of Revolutionary War origin, and these were all from the north end of the parade ground and the West Barracks. These pertained to the Second Battalion Pennsylvania, Continental Army; the First Battalion Pennsylvania, Continental Army (fig. 5.18); and the American Twenty-second Regiment. All of them may have come from soldiers passing through on their way to Canada in 1776, or else the soldiers may have been based at Mount Independence/Fort Ticonderoga in 1776–1777; however, another possibility is that they came from soldiers quarantined in the smallpox hospitals nearby, twenty years after the fort was gone.

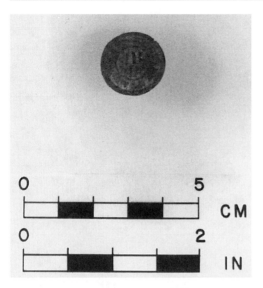

FIG. 5.18. A button of the First Battalion Pennsylvania, Continental Army, discovered inside the West Barracks at Fort William Henry.

Over one thousand fragments of English white-clay tobacco pipe stems were recovered from the recent excavations, along with several hundred bowl fragments. When coupled with the many thousands of pipes excavated in the 1950s, there is no denying that smoking must have been a favorite leisure activity at the fort. Some 653 (61%) of the pipe stem fragments were discovered in the dump at Site 5, and most of the remainder were found inside the West Barracks. A majority of the pipe stems had bore diameters of either 4/64 or 5/64 inch, very typical of mid- to late-eighteenth-century pipes (table 5.2).

It is known that the bores of eighteenth-century pipes typically shrank by 1/64 inch approximately every 38.26 years, so when these bore diameters are averaged, using the straight-line regression formula developed

Table 5.2
Tobacco Pipe Stem Fragments, 1997–2000
(Variations in Pipe Bore Diameters, in 1/64-inch Increments)

Diameter (inches)	Site 1	Site 2	Site 3	Site 4	Site 5	Site 6	Site 8	Site 9	Site 10	Site 13
3/64	0	0	0	0	0	0	6	0	0	2
4/64	13	3	1	59	424	10	152	4	1	0
5/64	6	8	0	79	227	9	60	2	0	0
6/64	1	0	0	0	2	0	2	0	0	0
Totals	20	11	1	138	653	19	220	6	1	2

FIG. 5.19. Examples of tobacco pipe bowls bearing the maker's mark, "R. TIPPET," discovered in the Site 5 dump (*left*) and at the north end of the parade ground (*right*).

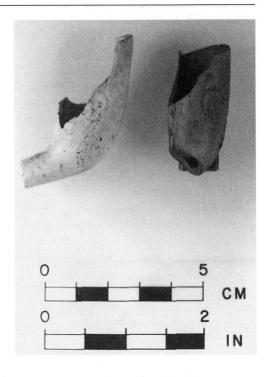

by the archeologist Lewis Binford, the total sample of 1,071 pipe stems have a mean date of 1764.77. This is clearly about eight years too late, since the known mean date for Fort William Henry is 1756. This is at first curious because so many frontier sites tend to have large numbers of "old," outdated artifacts, but the bore diameters may suggest something else. Because the pipe sample includes large numbers of "late" (4/64 inch) pipes, this may most easily be explained by a large occupation at or near the site during the Revolutionary War era. This has already been suggested by the three numbered regimental buttons and by the huge numbers of curious visitors who are known to have visited the charred ruins of the fort throughout the late eighteenth and nineteenth centuries.

The second method that may be used to date the tobacco pipes is to study the maker's marks on many of the bowls. Some of these marks are broken and incomplete, but clearly the most common maker of pipes supplied to Fort William Henry was R TIPPET (also appearing on a few pipes as RT). Three generations of Robert Tippets in Bristol, England, are known to have manufactured prodigious numbers of these pipes; they were very common during the French and Indian War (see fig. 5.19); and at least twelve pipes with this maker's mark were found in Sites 1, 4, and 5.

While only one example was found, a TD mark inside a cartouche with a ropelike edge was discovered very deep (100 to 104 inches, 255–

265 cm) within the Site 5 dump. This fragmentary pipe bowl was one of our most significant finds; previously, the earliest firmly dated TD pipe ever found in the region was one discovered by Paul Huey and Lois Feister at the 1758 site of Fort Gage, excavated in 1975. The Fort William Henry specimen was close to the bottom of a reasonably intact dump, so it appears to be earlier by one to three years.

Other maker's marks that we discovered on pipe bowls and stems included WM within a rouletted circle (the mark of the London maker William Mamby), a crown over 16, IW within a circle, CW, a thistle, a leafy plant, . . LBANY, CUTTY, and OLANDER. Some of these are definitely nineteenth-century maker's marks, further evidence that pipe-smoking visitors often strolled past what was left of the fort.

There also are several other distinctive categories of artifacts that should be mentioned, even though they were not present in great quantities. We found a total of eight British halfpennies and Spanish silver reals, although most were so worn that the dates could not be read; most were discovered inside the West Barracks and in the Site 5 dump. Evidence for sewing came chiefly from the West Barracks, where we recovered eighteen straight pins, one sewing needle, a pair of scissors, and one brass thimble (fig. 5.16), but there were small numbers of pins elsewhere, and a pair of scissors was found near the cemetery. And finally, the only evidence we discovered for musical instruments were two mouth harps (Jew's harps), both of which were found in the Site 5 dump. Neither had retained its metal "tongue" with which it would have produced its distinctive vibrating sound (fig. 5.20).

0   5
CM
0   2
IN

FIG. 5.20. A mouth harp (Jew's harp) discovered in the Site 5 dump.

Final Thoughts

Fort William Henry was occupied for only two years, but between the 1950s artifact collections and our own more recent work in the 1990s, archeology has recovered an exceptional number of artifacts from the ruins of the fort. Many pertain directly to the attack upon the fort in 1757, but a majority are the small objects from everyday life that were discarded when they wore out or broke. The fort's primary dump (Site 5) contained the largest quantities of almost everything, especially food remains, but there also was garbage scattered just about everywhere else, including inside the cellars of barracks and under the entire parade ground. It appears that little was wasted, and we found very few things that were still complete or functional.

Often a site that has been destroyed by fire may contain amazing examples of well-preserved artifacts that were not recovered soon afterward during salvage efforts. However, the British soldiers who departed Fort William Henry took many belongings with them, and it appears that almost everything else was stripped away by the French and Indians, who wanted spoils to take back to Fort Ticonderoga and Canada. We may have hoped to find cellar rooms that had caved in with all of their contents still intact, but such was not the case.

Chapter 6

Native People at Lake George before the Soldiers Arrived

The Prehistory of the Lake George Region

BEFORE THE eighteenth-century armies arrived at Lake George, the shores of the lake had long been home to small, intermittent settlements of Native Americans. These sites were highly seasonal, typically consisting of hunting and fishing camps, and probably not as rich as sites farther to the south, along the Hudson River. Still, food resources around Lake George would have seemed wonderfully inviting compared to sites located in the interior of the Adirondacks, just to the northwest (see the box "Indians in the Adirondacks").

Remarkably little research has been done on these prehistoric camps, even though local artifact collections, which contain many bifurcate-base projectile points, suggest that settlement on the Late Pleistocene terraces overlooking Lake George has been fairly dense since at least the Early Archaic period (ca. 8000–6000 B.C.). There is no evidence for Indians living locally during the earlier Paleo-Indian period (ca. 9500–8000 B.C.), just after glaciers retreated from northern New York State, although local drainage systems had probably become modern by about 12,000 years before the present. None of the distinctive fluted Clovis projectile points that typify the Paleo-Indian period has been found locally, although they certainly may eventually be found on the eastern side of the lake. After all, it took time for the climate to become fully modern, and probably the local vegetation and fauna were not rich enough to support a substantial population before the Early Archaic.

There is little evidence for occupation around Lake George during the Middle Archaic period (ca. 6000–4000 B.C.), perhaps because some aspect of the climate was not as well suited to human settlement at that time. A little bit later, during what is known as the Late Archaic (ca. 4000–1000 B.C.), prehistoric artifacts suddenly become more frequent around Lake George, suggesting that the population was beginning to

★ Indians in the Adirondacks

Just to the north and west of Lake George is the vast expanse of the Adirondack Mountains, now regulated by the Adirondack Park Agency, which restricts development and helps to ensure that the year-round population is light even today. Generally speaking, the region's biomass is fairly low, and throughout prehistory it would have been difficult for the pine-spruce forest to support a large Native population. In modern times the image has developed that Indians *never* lived in the Adirondacks, that it was just a hunting territory for the Iroquois or a buffer between the Iroquois and their Algonquian-speaking neighbors to the north. This model describes trails passing through the region, much used by raiding parties in the summer but without a significant year-round presence. Models proposed for early habitation in both the Green Mountains of Vermont and the White Mountains of New Hampshire are similar, and it is widely believed that the lower carrying capacity of upland areas ensured a marginal existence at best.

However, it is important to consider the changing ways by which Native people adjusted to available food resources. While the shores of Lake George and Lake Champlain would have offered more food and easier transportation, the interior of the Adirondacks would have supplied ample amounts of white-tailed deer, black bear, butternuts, hickory nuts, and other plant foods for Archaic period peoples. Archaic sites and artifacts have been found on lake shores in most of the modern towns in the region. Some of these were listed, by county, in Arthur C. Parker's *Archeological History of New York*, whereas William Ritchie's more modern *The Archaeology of New York State* neglected the Adirondacks almost completely.

Easily the best synthesis on Adirondack prehistory is Lynn Woods's "History in Fragments," an unusually complete guide to Adirondack sites and artifacts: it appeared in *Adirondack Life* magazine and featured interviews with many of those who have local artifact collections. Sites on Tupper Lake, Long Lake, the Raquette River, and elsewhere have revealed plenty of projectile points, as well as knives, scrapers, drills, and scatters of lithic debitage (flakes, cores, etc.)— the flakes left over from the manufacture and resharpening of tools. Pottery, suggestive of lengthier occupations in the Woodland Period, is exceptionally rare everywhere in the Adirondacks.

While a few sites appear fairly rich, more typically they are like the small site at the outlet from Friends Lake, where the Auringer-Seelye Chapter of the New York State Archaeological Association discovered a single Otter Creek projectile point and a mass of fire-cracked rocks from a campsite occupied for only a night or two. Such hunting camps created by family bands no doubt exist by the thousands, but given ten thousand years of human occupation, they need not mean more than a few dozen occupants in the whole of the Adirondacks at any given time.

Years ago, Joseph Caldwell of the Illinois State Museum coined the term "forest efficiency" to describe how Indian populations became so well adapted to this environment of forests, lakes, and streams that there was virtually no need to progress, to develop a new set of adaptations to an Eastern Woodland biomass that itself was not changing. However, as corn-beans-squash horticulture moved into southern New York State, deeper, richer soils along river floodplains became more desirable places to live, and the length of the growing season in the Adirondacks was just too brief for the requirements of corn. In the Archaic period the Adirondacks were almost as good for human habitation as were other regions, but in the Woodland period the area was downgraded to a hunting territory used by Indians living around its margins.

Thus, when Montcalm's army advanced upon Fort William Henry, it was through a relatively unpopulated region that probably had no permanent year-round villages. It was only on the northern side of the St. Lawrence River that good soils resulted in populous nations such as the Huron. Today only a few museums in the Adirondacks tell the story of Native Americans, most notably the Six Nations Museum in Onchiota, and there is but a single display case at the Adirondack Museum in Blue Mountain Lake.

mushroom, or at least that seasonal visits were increasing. Changing styles of projectile points now included the types known as Otter Creek, Vosburg, Lamoka, Brewerton, and Snook Kill. This was a period when hunting and fishing continued, along with gathering wild plants, but with probably a more complete adaptation to local forest and lake environments and with camps occupied for longer periods.

Still later, as the first pottery, horticulture, and a more settled lifestyle arrived in the region, archeologists use the term Woodland period to describe the next set of adaptations to local resources. In Lake George there is little evidence for the early part of the Woodland (ca. 1000–200 B.C.), but the middle (200 B.C.–A.D. 1000) and late (A.D. 1000–1500) Woodland are well represented, with a wide range of pottery styles, pendants or gorgets, and the distinctive projectile point types known as Jack's Reef and Levanna.

The earliest of the known sites in the Lake George area was researched by Dr. Dean Snow, at that time a professor at the State University at Albany (SUNY). In the late 1970s, Snow exposed Early Archaic artifacts at the Harrisena site, a temporary camp located at the northern end of a portage between the Hudson River and Lake George. In unusually deep soil layers, Snow found a mixture of bifurcate-base projectile points, Plano and Kirk points, and knives and scrapers, most of which had been manufactured from quartz and quartzite. Sites such as this provide evidence for hunting, butchering, and the working of hides but, according to Snow, no real evidence for fishing at the Harrisena site.

A small number of other projects have been conducted by professional archeologists in the Lake George area, including work by Dr. Robert Funk, who was New York State Archeologist from 1973 to 1993. Funk assisted Tom and Paul Weinman at the Weinman site on Assembly Point as they uncovered Late Archaic and late Middle Woodland artifacts between 1963 and 1966. The Weinmans, who are experienced avocational archeologists, have located and excavated several other sites along the edges of Lake George, including the Pickle Hill, Finley, Knox, and Denham sites.

Assuming each site was occupied for no more than a few nights before Indians reestablished themselves at other campsites, there may well be evidence for thousands of short-term Archaic and Woodland camps along the edges of Lake George. No more than a dozen or so have ever been professionally excavated, so there appears to be tremendous potential for future research.

Prehistoric Discoveries at Fort William Henry in the 1950s

Stanley Gifford was certainly not looking for a major prehistoric site when he arrived in Lake George in 1953, but his efforts uncovered thousands of prehistoric projectile points, pottery sherds, and ground-stone tools underlying the ruins of Fort William Henry. These ranged in time period from the Early Archaic through the Late Woodland, and according to Gifford, some were extremely deep:

> Twelve feet below the surface of the North West Bastion and six feet below the burned line of the fort, the earliest material was recovered. These artifacts consisted of small stemmed javelin points, flint scrapers and beach pebble net sinkers.

Several hundred of these artifacts are presently on display at the fort, in exhibits in both the West and North Barracks and also in the display area just inside the main entrance to the fort. Thousands of other prehistoric artifacts rest in boxes and cabinets in a storage room, cataloged and packed away by Gifford as he concluded his project.

While no records survive showing exactly where most of these artifacts were found, Gifford did describe finding a small pocket of burned bone from a human cremation burial covered with red ochre (powdered hematite). Associated with this was a ground-slate point, suggesting that the grave dated to the Middlesex Culture of the Early Woodland period. Fortunately, Carleton Dunn, who excavated at the fort with Gifford, remembers that the shallow burial was found outside the northeast bastion of the reconstructed fort, where it was examined by William Ritchie, the New York State Archeologist at that time. Dunn also remembers that they unearthed four flexed prehistoric skeletons some 100 or 150 feet northeast of what is now the Trolley Restaurant on Canada Street; these were later reburied off the property in a ceremony supervised by Native Americans. Elsewhere, Gifford found hearths, clusters of lithic cache blades (fig. 6.1), post molds, and even pieces of charred corn and beans.

The artifacts that survive in storage are the best guide to the time levels that Gifford was digging through, and lithic tools include an un-

FIG. 6.1. Stanley Gifford exposing a cache of prehistoric blades. Fort William Henry Museum.

usually large sample of early bifurcate-base projectile points (the Early Archaic), Otter Creek, Vosburg, Brewerton, Lamoka, Snook Kill, and Orient Fishtail points (the Late Archaic), Jack's Reef Corner-Notched points (the Middle Woodland), and Levanna and Madison points (the Late Woodland). Ground-stone axes were common (fig. 6.2), as were net sinkers, pendants, hammerstones, and virtually thousands of pottery sherds. Gifford even found a single fragment from a ground-slate knife, or *ulu* (fig. 6.3).

A majority of the prehistoric pottery found underneath the fort dates to the Point Peninsula series of the Middle Woodland period, including the types known as Point Peninsula Plain, Wickham Corded, Wickham Incised, Wickham Punctate (fig. 6.4), Jack's Reef Corded, Vinette

Dentate, and St. Lawrence Pseudo Scallop Shell. Later, from the Late Woodland period, there are a small number of Early Owasco sherds. Perhaps what makes the large quantity of pottery most interesting is that it implies a fairly settled population here, with farming being practiced nearby. Significantly, that means the Indians visiting Lake George did not rely solely upon resources from the lake.

FIG. 6.2. Ground-stone axes recovered from Fort William Henry in the 1950s.

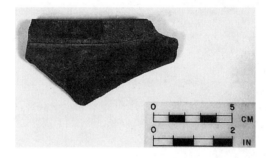

FIG. 6.3. A slate *ulu* recovered from Fort William Henry in the 1950s.

FIG. 6.4. Sherds of Wickham Punctate recovered from Fort William Henry in the 1950s.

Recent Prehistoric Finds

In 1995 an excavation was conducted in the cemetery area outside the
fort by anthropologists Maria Liston and Brenda Baker during the filming of a *New Detectives* show for the Discovery Channel. This work
uncovered four bifurcate-base projectile points of the Kanawha and St.
Albans types, suggesting an occupation in this area by at least 6000 B.C.
Later projectile point types found near the cemetery included Neville
(Middle Archaic) and Fox Creek (Middle Woodland) points, and there
were numerous pottery sherds from several vessels made during the
Middle and Late Woodland periods. Given the presence of two or three
small hearths as well, which produced carbon-14 dates of A.D. 960 and
A.D. 1640, it is clear that the area southwest of the fort has been a popu-
lar occupation site for at least 8,000 years.

Given the quantities of artifacts found by Gifford, followed by the
1995 work, we knew that our own excavations at the fort between 1997
and 2000 were guaranteed to add even more to this rich prehistoric
record. It was no surprise, then, that we found Native American artifacts
scattered almost everywhere the soldiers had camped. Interpreting exactly where many artifacts originated was difficult, though, because of
the disturbed nature of so much of the fort. Dirt had constantly been
shifted as soldiers dug cellars, latrines, and such, bringing earlier artifacts up to the surface. Other artifacts were brought in with sand from
the beach below, creating the sand-filled walls of the fort. And still others
were moved about during the 1950s reconstruction. The result is that
almost every spear point or sherd we found had previously been moved,
and Indian artifacts from several thousand years ago now rested side by
side with the residue of European civilization. The only way to sort out
the fort's prehistory, then, had to be by comparison of our finds to better
stratified, more datable artifacts at other sites.

Inside the reconstructed fort, underneath the northern end of the
parade ground (Sites 4 and 8), our four years of excavations have uncovered extensive scatters of prehistoric pottery from both the Middle and
Late Woodland periods (fig. 6.5). Ironically, these sherds lie just inches
underneath the surface where soldiers walked in the eighteenth century,
probably unaware that Indians had occupied the very same space a thousand years before them. According to Robert Funk and Louise Basa,
who have examined the newly discovered sherds, most of this pottery
dates to the late Middle Woodland, and they include the styles and types
of decoration known as Vinette Dentate, Pseudo-Scallop Shell, and
Rocker-Impressed Pseudo-Scallop Shell. The Late Woodland sherds
are decorated with much incising, and some appear to be from vessels

with collars, the name given to a raised area around the rim that contains the decoration.

The stone tools found beneath the parade ground include a Brewerton Side-notched point, a Fishtail point, and a Jack's Reef Corner-notched point. Perhaps the most surprising find in the parade was a small but very intact hearth of fire-cracked rocks that we found in 1997, just west of the 1756 well and only about a foot below the crushed rocks that tourists walk on today.

Of all the excavations we have conducted inside the fort, we have found the deepest soil disturbances within the West Barracks (Site 8), where soldiers inadvertently mixed artifacts together as they dug the cellar of the barracks down to a depth of about eight feet. It was there that our field supervisor, Matthew Rozell, found a bifurcate-base projectile point and a base from another, of the type known as "Kanawha" (fig. 6.6), as well as large, bifacially flaked preforms or knives (fig. 6.7); later point styles, including Brewerton Eared-notched, Brewerton Side-notched, and Vosburg; and Middle Woodland pottery, all mixed together with the remains of soldiers' garbage. In a good example of "reverse stratigraphy," the oldest spear points were actually the shallowest, located within two feet of the surface.

Just outside the eastern wall of the reconstructed fort, in the dumping area we termed Site 5, we made a spectacular prehistoric discovery in 1998. Some six feet (180 cm) deep, overlain with a few dozen sherds of

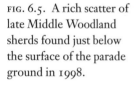

FIG. 6.5. A rich scatter of late Middle Woodland sherds found just below the surface of the parade ground in 1998.

FIG. 6.6. Examples of pre-historic artifacts excavated between 1997 and 2000. *Top:* rocker-stamped rim sherd (late Middle Woodland) and two-hole slate gorget fragment (Middle Woodland).
Bottom: corner-notched Middle Woodland point of brown jasper, bifurcate-base point of rhyolite, and bifurcate-base point fragment of rhyolite.

FIG. 6.7. Large bifaces excavated from the West Barracks foundation (Site 8), manufactured from quartzite and shale.

incised pottery, was a gigantic stone feature—what archeologists often term a roasting or smoking platform (fig. 6.8). Composed of hundreds of fire-cracked rocks and measuring 6.9 by 5.25 feet, this giant pavement was probably used for smoking or drying fish caught in Lake George. It would have taken only a minute to walk up from the shore to the sandy terrace above the lake, carrying the day's catch, and to cook or smoke the fish.

Just north of the roasting platform, side by side with garbage from the fort, our crews spent three summers, under the direction of Andrew Farry and Brad Jarvis, uncovering literally hundreds of prehistoric tools and sherds. These included fragments of two Middle Woodland gorgets or pendants (fig. 6.6), a Middle Woodland corner-notched point of brown jasper (fig. 6.6), a Madison point, and a Fox Creek point variant.

FIG. 6.8. The large roasting platform of fire-cracked rocks discovered underneath the soldiers' dump (Site 5). The scale points north and is marked in 10-cm units.

The pottery found within the dump was chiefly late Middle Woodland in date and included Wickham Incised, rocker-stamped sherds (fig. 6.6), sherds from collared vessels, and dentate sherds.

Our own excavations within the fort's cemetery did not produce the same quantities of prehistoric artifacts that Liston and Baker encountered in 1995. Still, teams led by Susan Winchell-Sweeney tested throughout the cemetery and modern parking lot where they encountered scatters of chert and quartz flakes, suggesting that the entire glacial terrace had been home to revolving groups of Native Americans. They returned again and again to camp on the sandy soil that provides such an excellent view of Lake George.

Historic Indians on Lake George

Stanley Gifford believed in the 1950s that Native Americans had lived on the edge of Lake George right up until the arrival of the European armies. Our own work has recovered virtually no contact-period artifacts to support this, and it seems doubtful that any Native settlement had stood on the site of Fort William Henry just prior to William Eyre's construction of the fort in late 1755.

In early historic times it was the Mohicans (or Mahicans) who lived on the eastern side of New York State, occupying the waterways that lie between New York State and Vermont. Ironically, James Fenimore Cooper appears to have confused the Mohicans of New York with the Mohegans of southeastern Connecticut who lived on the Thames River near New London. This is especially apparent in his selection of the name Uncas for one of his heroes in *The Last of the Mohicans*. Uncas was the name of a prominent Mohegan sachem in Connecticut, with no direct connection to the Mohicans of New York.

The Mohicans lived along the upper and middle drainage area of the Hudson River, from the southern shores of Lake Champlain down to the Catskill Mountains and east into the Berkshires of Massachusetts. Altogether, there were about five thousand of them when they greeted Henry Hudson during his voyage up the Hudson River in 1609. We do not know whether most of the prehistoric artifacts that have been found on Lake George were made by the direct ancestors of the Mohicans of early historic times, but that is perhaps the most likely interpretation. A few artifacts that may have Iroquois associations, especially pottery sherds with Iroquois-style decoration and triangular Madison projectile points, have been found on the edges of Lake George, and these were probably dropped by hunters or war parties that were quickly passing through.

It was thus at the very end of thousands of years of sporadic occupation that Indians from many different nations converged upon Fort William Henry in August of 1757. Some of the Indians on the British side were Mohican (or "Stockbridge") Indians (see the box "The Mohicans Today"), and these were among the first to be captured or slain during the massacre on August 10. On the French side, Indians from as many as thirty-three different nations in eastern Canada and the upper Great Lakes journeyed to Lake George in the summer of 1757 to obtain scalps and plunder from the British. These included representatives of the Huron, Abenaki, Algonkin, Potawatomi, Ottawa, Iroquois, Nipissing, Ojibwa, Mississauga, Menominee, Winnebago, Sauk, Amalicite, Fox, Iowa, Loup, Puant, Delaware, Micmac, and others.

★ The Mohicans Today

There are extremely few Mohicans living within their former tribal territory, but originally they were the dominant power in eastern New York State. Their villages were surrounded by stockades and were usually located on hilltops for defense, but it was necessary to move every eight to twelve years as farmland and firewood became exhausted. T. J. Brasser has estimated that village populations averaged about two hundred persons and has written that Mohican longhouses each had an average of three fireplaces (and therefore at least three families). The Mohicans typically relied upon horticulture and fishing, with the women planting and tending the crops, while men fished, gathered mussels, and hunted.

From a peak population of 5,000 or 5,300 in the early 1600s, the Mohicans' numbers were radically reduced by warfare and disease. Dean Snow has estimated that a mortality rate of 91 percent dropped their population to about five hundred by A.D. 1700. Their decline in numbers, prompting a move into refugee communities, caused the Mohawk to claim much of the Mohican territory as their own during the seventeenth and eighteenth centuries. There have been subsequent efforts to claim that this was *always* Mohawk land, but that simply is not the case. With the passage of time, the Mohicans did not die out altogether, but their small numbers caused them to become increasingly marginalized.

In 1734 the Mohicans founded Stockbridge, Massachusetts, as a Christian town, and they built a meetinghouse, church, school, and houses much like those of the Europeans. It was then that they became known as the Stockbridge Indians, and they subsequently aligned themselves with Rogers' Rangers during the French and Indian War, fighting against some of the tribes in eastern Canada. Later, during the American Revolution, all of them fought on the side of the American colonists. Many then traveled west to Indiana to join their cousins, the Miami, and others went to Wisconsin in the 1780s, where they still occupy a small reservation.

While Mohicans are now spread all across the United States, very few have chosen to return to their native lands, and regrettably their language is dead because the last speaker of that language died early in the twentieth century. One of the few to return home is Steve Comer, a resident of Sand Lake, New York, and a grandson of the last Mohican speaker. Today, Steve is often called upon to speak for his people in New York State and is fighting to keep their memory alive and participating in reburial ceremonies whenever a Native American grave is found within the Mohican territory. It must be a rather lonely legacy, knowing that his people are best remembered because of a novel written in 1826!

Many of those who took part did so because they had learned of the French victory over the British forts at Oswego the previous year and hoped to achieve an equally dramatic victory. It was an unwieldy group, some of whom were traditional enemies, and the French needed several translators in order to converse in such a great variety of languages. Because some had traveled 1,500 miles and more, coming from many parts of Canada, they spread smallpox over a vast area when they returned home. Ironically, this had been one of the greatest gatherings of warriors from disparate Indian nations that ever occurred in American history, yet their success proved remarkably short-lived.

After the end of the colonial wars, the Native presence in the Lake George area was minimal until the turn of the twentieth century. At that time, Abenaki and Iroquois basketmakers regularly visited Lake George to sell beadwork, baskets, and birchbark items to summer visitors. Although the annual summer trade has ended, Abenaki customs are remembered and advanced by the prominent Abenaki storyteller Joseph Bruchac and his family, who live only about twenty miles to the south in Wilton, New York.

Chapter 7

Surviving Landmarks from the Eighteenth Century

Revisiting the Past

ONE OF THE BEST reasons for reading *The Last of the Mohicans* is to enjoy James Fenimore Cooper's wonderful gift for creating sites, events, and landscapes that are so detailed you can truly see the action. Throughout the story it is easy to imagine that you are really watching the canoes gliding over the water, that you are staring up at the solitary sentries patrolling the walls of Fort William Henry, or that you are part of Hawkeye's band hiding inside Cooper's Cave, awaiting discovery by the Hurons. But one of the more enjoyable outcomes of reading a historical novel is that afterward you can actually visit the sites you have read about and compare the reality with what you have been imagining.

It has been over 170 years since Cooper visited many of the sites that figure prominently in his story, and over 240 years have passed since the siege and massacre at Fort William Henry. The original log forts have rotted away, highways lie alongside the old Indian paths, most of the forests have been cut down, and Lake George is ringed with restaurants and tourist beaches. It takes a bit of effort to rediscover the historical sites, but they *are* there, and visitors to the region may still delight in traveling in Hawkeye's (and Cooper's) footsteps.

Fort Edward

The Last of the Mohicans begins with General Webb and the British army stationed in Fort Edward, and travelers may profitably visit the modern village of Fort Edward and walk around the edges of the fort site. Cooper makes little effort to describe the fort, but he does comment on General Webb's residence because it was from there that Colonel

Monro's daughters were getting set to depart for Lake George and Fort William Henry: "But there still remained the signs of another departure, before a log cabin of unusual size and accommodations, in front of which those sentinels paced their rounds who were known to guard the person of the English general."

Clearly Cooper was not greatly interested in the companion fort to Fort William Henry; after all, it was not the site of a massacre, and its commander, General Webb, had failed to relieve Fort William Henry when help was sorely needed. Unlike its sister fort, Fort Edward was not destroyed by fire; instead, early settlers apparently removed and reused a lot of what remained. All that is left today to identify the fort are a few signs placed behind the Anvil Restaurant, although surface contours help to identify where the moat was originally located. Fort Edward saw some archeology in 1995 and 1996, but there has been no reconstruction, and there are no outdoor exhibits. However, it is possible to visit the Fort House Museum at the southern end of the village and the Rogers Island Visitors Center on an island in the Hudson River; both have pertinent exhibits and a few artifacts from the fort.

Cooper's Cave

As Hawk-eye and his companions set out for Lake George, they journeyed along trails that can no longer be identified but by now must be covered over with houses and blacktop. They emerged at the Hudson River and traveled by canoe to a small island at the base of Glens Falls (which was not given that name until 1788); there they hid from their Indian pursuers in a cavern:

> The rock proved softer on each side of us, and so they left the center of the river bare and dry, first working out these two little holes for us to hide in.
> "We are then on an island?"
> "Aye! There are the falls on two sides of us, and the river above and below. If you had daylight, it would be worth the trouble to step up on the height of this rock, and look at the perversity of the water. It falls by no rule at all; sometimes it leaps, sometimes it tumbles; there, it skips; here, it shoots; in one place 'tis white as snow, and in another 'tis green as grass; hereabouts, it pitches into deep hollows, that rumble and quake the 'arth; and thereaway, it ripples and sings like a brook, fashioning whirlpools and gulleys in the old stone, as it 'twas no harder than trodden clay. The whole design of the river seems disconcerted."

This was the site that has been known as Cooper's Cave ever since Cooper visited there in 1825 and gave it such prominent attention in his story.

FIG. 7.1. An early view of Cooper's Cave: "Falls of the Hudson River at Glens Falls, Warren County" by Seneca Ray Stoddard. Courtesy of the Lake George Historical Association.

The limestone cave had been hollowed out by water, making it an ideal hiding place, and Cooper visited it during a low-water period, when it was somewhat larger. The novel caused Cooper's Cave to become a popular destination for guided tours, and nineteenth-century photographers such as Seneca Ray Stoddard publicized it further (fig. 7.1).

Unfortunately, late-nineteenth-century blasting for a cast-iron truss bridge that connected Glens Falls with South Glens Falls caused some damage to the roof of the cave, and it has not been easy to see from the current bridge that carries Route 9 over the river. A spiral concrete staircase, thirty-five feet high, with about fifty steps, was built in December 1914 and made it possible to descend from the bridge to the cave below. This was in use until 1961, at which time the staircase was torn down. However, the site, which is owned by Niagara Mohawk Power Corporation, is anything but forgotten, and several local organizations have taken their names from this attraction: the Cooper's Cave Coin and Stamp Club, Cooper's Cave Ale Company, Cooper's Cave Auto Club, Cooper's Cave Federal Credit Union, and others.

New interest in the cave has been growing over the past few years, and there has been a highly publicized effort to provide public access and to turn the cave into a unique type of tourist attraction. It may not be easy to reach the cave safely with a walkway from the south side of the river or via an elevator from the Route 9 bridge; still, if public enthusiasm prevails, the New York State Department of Transportation (DOT) will soon find a way to create access as it replaces the bridge overhead. However, the challenge for the DOT is more daunting than in Cooper's day. The limestone rocks are very slippery, and Cooper did not have to worry about issues of liability and handicapped accessibility.

Lake George

While in the cave, Hawk-eye's party was captured by Magua and his band of Hurons, although not until after Hawk-eye, Uncas, and Chingachgook managed to escape by leaping into the Hudson River. Later, after being reunited, Hawkeye and his companions traveled north toward Lake George, no doubt passing by the spot where Colonel Ephraim Williams had been killed two years earlier, in 1755. Today there is a stone marker honoring Williams's memory on the east side of Route 9, a little bit west of where he fell; this was installed by Williams College in 1854, in tribute to the leader whose bequest helped to found the college.

A mile further to the north on the military road, Hawk-eye passed by Bloody Pond, where many French and Indians had been killed during the battle of Lake George. Cooper made Hawk-eye an integral part of that battle by making him the guide for the New Hampshire soldiers who surprised two hundred French and Indians by the side of a small pond:

> "Just hereaway, where you see the trees rise into a mountain swell, I met a party coming down to our aid, and I led them where the enemy were taking their meal, little dreaming that they had not finished the bloody work of the day."
>
> "And you surprised them?"
>
> "If death can be a surprise to men who are thinking only of the cravings of their appetites. We gave them but little breathing time, for they had borne hard upon us in the fight of the morning, and there were few in our party who had not lost friend or relative by their hands. When all was over, the dead, and some say the dying, were cast into that little pond. These eyes have seen its waters colored with blood, as natural water never yet flowed from the bowels of the 'arth."

There now is a boulder on the east side of Route 9 that identifies Bloody Pond, although the present pond that is visible from the highway is some distance west of the original Bloody Pond.

As they traveled along, Hawk-eye also commented on the site of the main action during the battle of Lake George, where General William Johnson defeated the French army under Baron Dieskau:

> "Hundreds of Frenchmen saw the sun that day for the last time; and even their leader, Dieskau himself, fell into our hands, so cut and torn with the lead that he has gone back to his own country, unfit for further acts in war."

The French defeat in 1755 occurred within what is now the Lake George Battlefield Park, where the thirteen-foot-high Lake George Battle Monument, erected in 1903 by the Society of Colonial Wars, depicts William Johnson and King Hendrick of the Mohawks (fig. 7.2). Here at the south end of Lake George, close to the earlier battle site, Hawk-eye passed by and commented upon the entrenched camp that was occupied by nearly two thousand British soldiers and militia in August of 1757. Two years later, it also became the site of Fort George and its dozens of barracks, huts, and hospitals.

The Lake George Battlefield Park is one of the very best places in which to get a feel for what Hawk-eye and his friends might have seen as they journeyed toward Fort William Henry. Managed by the New York State Department of Environmental Conservation, the park is heavily wooded, yet its surface is covered with great numbers of foundations dating to the 1750s. Among its attractions are a bronze statue of a Native American, dedicated in 1921, and the ruins of the southwest bastion of Fort George (figs. 7.3 and 7.4). Nothing has been reconstructed, although the fort's bastion has seen some stabilization in the twentieth century.

FIG. 7.2. The Lake George Battle Monument (1903) in Lake George Battlefield Park, portraying General Sir William Johnson and King Hendrick of the Mohawks.

Various sites throughout the park are now being studied archeologically (see the box "Recent Excavations in Lake George Battlefield Park"), and with time it will be possible to determine exactly the location of the battle of Lake George, to find the site of the entrenched camp of 1757, and to discover where General Amherst erected many of his army's buildings in 1759. This beautiful park and campground is a "must see" for visitors who are tracing the route of *The Last of the Mohicans*, and the tour road that passes through the park has signage identifying many of the sites. Also, the Beach House, located just to the north on the state's "Million Dollar Beach," contains exhibits featuring the many military sites located in the park.

Fort William Henry

The destination of Hawkeye's little party was, of course, Fort William Henry, and the most memorable passages in *The Last of the Mohicans* must surely be those in which Cooper describes the siege and subsequent massacre at the fort. Those who have read about Fort William Henry and now wish to see it can view a reasonably correct reconstruction on the original site, albeit set against the very modern village of Lake George; in effect, the availability of original construction plans from 1755, combined with extensive archeology, have helped to make this reconstruction more accurate than most. The only noticeable limitations in the reconstruction are (1) two barracks were reconstructed, the West and the North, rather than the four barracks that existed in the 1750s;

FIG. 7.3. The southwest bastion of Fort George in 1895, before any stabilization or brush clearing. Courtesy of the Village of Lake George.

FIG. 7.4. The southwest bastion of Fort George after stabilization and clearing, probably in the 1910s. Courtesy of the Lake George Historical Association.

(2) the original wooden cribs that made up the walls of the fort were filled in with sand and stones, to absorb the impact of cannonfire, whereas the cribwork of the reconstruction is open (and is currently used for storage); and (3) the original fort sat on the very edge of Lake George, but the water has receded since then, causing the present reconstruction to sit a few hundred feet from the shore. While it was important to rebuild the fort on its original site, it *is* rather confusing to find it sitting now so far from the water.

Visitors to Lake George may readily visualize and understand British defenses simply by entering Fort William Henry; however, it is regrettable that the French entrenchments and camps in the village of Lake George have been built over. Only a few historic markers exist, and those give only a very general sense of where the French were positioned at the time of the siege.

Since its opening in 1956, the reconstruction of the fort has had its own colorful history, and hundreds of college students have helped with the interpretation each summer. Many of the original exhibits from the

★ Recent Excavations in Lake George Battlefield Park

The summer of the year 2000 marked the beginning of archeological fieldwork within Lake George Battlefield Park, the last major untouched military site in the corridor that runs from New York City to Canada. Our team from Adirondack Community College, led by Andrew Farry and Brad Jarvis, dug into the foundations of two of the barracks buildings that General Amherst constructed there in 1759, as well as several lesser sites. In the process they discovered amazingly well preserved walls and tremendous numbers of artifacts from both the French and Indian War and the American Revolution. Both building foundations were solidly constructed of mortared limestone, and the overlying soil was often two feet thick or more. This buried the

foundations much deeper than expected, at a site where the natural bedrock juts through the surface of the battlefield in many places. The presence of deeply buried foundations made this one of the richest military sites we have ever seen.

Both foundations were located inside what was formerly a wooden stockade of three bastions at the northern edge of a high bluff that overlooks Lake George; in modern times, the famed Million Dollar Beach lies just below. From historical maps we know that this fortification contained two small barracks buildings and was the front line of defense while the main fort, Fort George, was being constructed about six hundred feet to the south. The more northerly foundation measured seventeen by sixty-seven feet

The Lake George Battlefield Park: Excavating inside the more southerly foundation (Site 2) in the summer of 2000. This foundation had long been identified by New York State as the site of a hospital, but it is more likely to have supported a barracks building. The scale board is graduated in 10-cm units.

The Lake George Battlefield Park: Mapping the walls of the more northerly foundation (Site 1) in the summer of 2000. The foundation wall on the right is four feet thick, and the interior wall at the bottom left is two feet thick. This foundation contained large amounts of wall plaster, suggesting higher-status occupants.

and inside we discovered great quantities of fallen wall plaster, suggesting that it may have been the officers' barracks. The second foundation, more ordinary in appearance, may have housed the enlisted men. We also found sherds of white, salt-glazed stoneware; delft; buff-bodied, slip-decorated earthenware; creamware; thousands of animal bones from the soldiers' meals, including fish bones from Lake George; many buttons, including numbered regimental buttons; a four-pound cannonball; musket parts; hinges; wine bottles; medicine bottles; gold braid; a complete spade; and much more.

The Lake George Battlefield Park has dozens of foundations scattered across its surface, and it is blessed with an absolutely spectacular view of Lake George. But above all, it has integrity. Its foundations contain artifacts that represent only twenty years, and little else is mixed in. Many of the artifacts that we have recovered so far appear to date to the French and Indian War, but the regimental buttons and the sherds of creamware demonstrate that the buildings were still in use during the Revolution.

The Lake George Battlefield Park encompasses events that occurred between the 1750s and the 1770s, and archeology is only just beginning to reveal its enormous potential to become one of the finest eighteenth-century military

sites in the nation. It showcases a major battle and is the only fort in Lake George that spans two wars; it includes barracks and lesser buildings and perhaps smallpox hospitals—all within an attractive setting. And best of all, it has not yet been destroyed by treasure hunters.

With the excavations now completed at Fort William Henry, we hope to spend the next several years determining the settlement patterning within this exciting military camp. British military maps show many of the buildings that surrounded Fort George, yet most of these still must be located on the ground. At the Lake George Battlefield Park, archeology is now the best way to interpret what has survived and to tell visitors a livelier and more complete story.

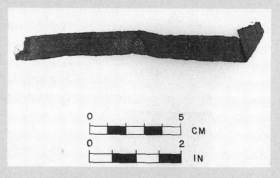

The Lake George Battlefield Park: Gold braid discovered in Site 2 in the summer of 2000.

FIG. 7.5. The West Barracks at Fort William Henry after the fire in 1967. Fort William Henry Museum.

1950s are still in place, but they are gradually being replaced with more modern displays. There are plenty of opportunities to see artifacts excavated from the ruins by Stanley Gifford, even though some of the best were lost in the fire that destroyed the West Barracks in 1967 (fig. 7.5). School groups, overseas visitors, boy scouts (fig. 7.6), weekenders from New York City and elsewhere, all generate a flood of activity in the summertime. Easily the busiest day each year is the Fourth of July, when three thousand to four thousand visitors enter the fort. It is almost like experiencing the siege all over again!

Traveling North from Lake George

After the massacre, Hawk-eye and his companions canoed north on Lake George, attempting to rescue Colonel Monro's daughters from Magua and his band of warriors as they traveled to the villages of Magua's people. It is in the northern forests that Cooper's narrative becomes vague as to locations and destinations, suggesting that Cooper was not overly familiar with the routes north of Lake George. This makes it difficult

FIG. 7.6. Boy Scout Day at Fort William Henry in 1959. Fort William Henry Museum.

FIG. 7.7. A modern (1999) view of the West Barracks at Fort William Henry.

to visit the more northerly sites, the dense, primeval forest described by Cooper, including the rocks and precipices where Uncas and Cora met their end at the hands of the Hurons.

However, the one northern site that must be visited to complete the story of *The Last of the Mohicans* is surely Fort Ticonderoga, the French stronghold from which Montcalm set out to attack Fort William Henry and to which he returned with his spoils of war. It is curious that Cooper did not include a visit to Ticonderoga in the latter stages of his story, especially since Cooper himself was there in 1825; instead, both pursuers and pursued journeyed straight to Indian villages in Canada. All the same, the French perspective on what happened at Fort William Henry is best understood by viewing the exhibits at Fort Ticonderoga and thereby better appreciating French efforts to hold onto their claims to Lake Champlain and Lake George.

Chapter 8

Conclusions

General Thoughts

A<small>N ARCHEOLOGICAL DIG</small> is rather like a good detective story—full of surprises, lots of unexpected twists, and lots of optimism that the ending will justify all the painstaking research. When I set out to dig the ruins of Fort William Henry in 1997, I did not know whether we would discover anything intact on the sandy terrace that overlooks Lake George or anything new that could be said about a 244-year-old murder story that is indelibly printed in our national consciousness. Still, I considered the site of Fort William Henry to be so significant in American colonial history that it almost didn't matter what we did or didn't find. It was a privilege to have the opportunity to dig there.

Thinking back, I remember that the first time I read *The Last of the Mohicans*, I was preparing a book report about a site that I had visited in the 1950s with my classmates. In that first reading, I accepted Cooper's novel as an old-fashioned adventure story written in rather archaic language; but it told a lively tale, so I enjoyed it. I believed that it was historically accurate, but I am not sure whether that mattered to me at the time.

Thirty-odd years later, my perceptions have changed, both about the book and about the site. The events that took place at Fort William Henry in 1757 were tragic and fatal for many, and I feel that obligates all of us to tell the story as accurately as possible; that is why movie versions of *The Last of the Mohicans* are often irritating, given their ability to create new myths about the past.

I cannot help but be impressed at the very significant role the fort played in French-British relations in the eighteenth century, in cementing European hatred and distrust toward Native Americans, and in causing the subsequent deaths of tens of thousands of Native people who had contracted smallpox. And above all, I am impressed by the long list of early Americans who were either stationed at the south end of Lake George or at least visited there. Paul Revere, Benedict Arnold, and

George Washington immediately come to mind. General Washington, for example, dismounted from his horse while inspecting the site in August 1783, walked through the ruins, and commented: "There is a lot of history under this ground." Millions of living Americans are descended from the soldiers and officers who served at Lake George, so this history is relevant to many.

I am not one of those who is bothered by James Fenimore Cooper's inability to adhere closely to the facts in *The Last of the Mohicans*. Cooper never pretended to be a historian, and he was writing for a popular audience. He was a storyteller, clearly writing a novel that he hoped would become as popular as English novels of his day, and the recording of dry facts would not have sold his book. Modern readers can certainly appreciate Cooper's insertion of sympathetic characters like Cora and Alice into his novel to liven up the story and the creation of Hawkeye to represent the basic goodness of pioneers in the new land. I personally feel that the criticisms of Cooper as a writer are excessive and that Mark Twain in particular was unusually petty and combative in making fun of Cooper's ability as a writer. Cooper's success with *The Last of the Mohicans* was immediate, and there are few other stories of the early nineteenth century that have endured as well.

Looking back on the events of August 1757, it is easy to have strong opinions about the relative merits—as leaders and as men—of Webb, Montcalm, and Monro. As the three principals who guided the action at Fort William Henry, their choices directly led to the battle, the victory/ defeat, and the massacre.

Monro, as a veteran officer on the front line, appears to have acted credibly throughout: he did not abandon his hopeless position; he resisted the French attack for a reasonable period of time; he obtained good terms of surrender for his men; and on the face of it, he was blameless for the massacre that followed (see the box "Who's to Blame?").

Webb, his superior officer, may or may not have been a coward, but his judgment must be questioned. Given the size of the advancing French army, which was well known, Webb should either have committed *all* of his troops immediately to the battle in Lake George or else abandoned Fort William Henry and pulled his men back to the stronger position in Fort Edward. By merely sending a token number of reinforcements to the relief of Fort William Henry, he was choosing to sacrifice half of the men under his command to save the other half. This was much too high a price, and Webb should have realized that the only one he appeared to be saving was himself. History does not remember Webb fondly, and I believe that negative assessment is correct.

The role of the Marquis de Montcalm is certainly the most interesting in all of this because of the similar situation he had faced upon

★ Who's to Blame?

The passage of time does not make it easier to accept the massacre at Fort William Henry, and many still care passionately about where to place the blame. The English soldiers and provincial militia were occupying a strategic position at the southern end of Lake George that had not been occupied by Mohicans in the recent past and where the French had never established a legitimate claim by virtue of a permanent settlement. The English *had* been provocative toward the French forces around Fort Carillon, but they had inflicted minimal casualties and probably did not pose an imminent danger to the French. During the siege at Fort William Henry the English had honorably surrendered on the expectation of safe passage to Fort Edward, and eighteenth-century rules of war should have protected all of them, including the sick and injured who were left behind inside the fort.

It has sometimes been claimed that the English made a mistake by not emptying the rum from their canteens because that gave the Indians an excuse to attack them. However, had the French given their prisoners even the tiniest bit of protection, this would not have been an issue. The English forces based in Lake George really cannot be blamed for the events that transpired, even if General Webb *can* be blamed for not doing more to rescue them.

While the French role in these events began well enough, they appear to have been exceptionally naive in believing that 1,600 Native warriors would blindly accept French authority and would tolerate terms of surrender that left them with no spoils of war. At the time of surrender, the chiefs had promised that their braves would accept the terms, but the French should have understood that war chiefs could not control the actions of braves with the same level of authority wielded by the French monarchy. Chiefs could coax and persuade but not command. Naïveté became culpability, however, when the French failed to restrain braves from entering the fort on August 9, failed to protect the integrity of the entrenched camp on August 10, and failed to protect the retreating column later on the 10th. This repeated unwillingness to uphold the peace terms, especially in light of the massacre at Oswego just a year earlier, strongly indicates French indifference to English life and property, and the French richly deserve the blame that has been given them by past authors. While there were individual Frenchmen, including Montcalm himself and Père Pierre Roubaud, who did act with compassion to save English prisoners from Indian captivity, this does not really compensate for French policies that failed to show proper respect for the rules of war.

Finally, it is most difficult to accept or justify the actions of Montcalm's Indian allies, and it is gratuitous to suggest that they simply were entitled to booty that the French and English would have denied them. The large Native American contingent attached to Montcalm's army was there precisely because of the easy victory and rewards at Oswego, and the English prisoners were viewed as "property" with a high value in Canada. The Indians were fully aware of the surrender terms, chose not to observe them, and showed neither courage nor honor in attacking and slaying the unarmed sick, injured, women, and children and even mutilating the dead in the military cemetery. Nor can they be credited merely with overzealousness in support of the French cause, because large numbers immediately began their return to Canada as soon as they had prisoners to take with them. The inconstancy of these allies was a key factor in Montcalm's decision not to proceed to attack Fort Edward.

In retrospect, then, Montcalm's Indian allies

became a powerful psychological inducement for the English to surrender, and their presence in the woods between Lake George and Fort Edward played a role in dissuading Webb from sending reinforcements. Unfortunately, their subsequent actions made this a hollow victory, stripping Montcalm of the glory that he should have enjoyed after the French victory.

capturing the British forts in Oswego the previous year. To be responsible for one massacre of British prisoners under his protection may perhaps be excused by Montcalm's ignorance of Native customs. But when he failed to give adequate protection to his prisoners at Fort William Henry, sending an escort of only a few hundred French regulars to accompany over two thousand unarmed soldiers and civilians, he alone created the conditions that brought about the massacre. Even though he personally facilitated the recovery from the Indians of four hundred prisoners before they could be taken to Canada, the responsibility for the massacre was his.

Finally, it must be asked whether recent research that has tended to shrink the number of British casualties during the massacre has also led to a downplaying of the culpability of Native Americans in the massacre. On the one hand, it certainly is appropriate to determine as precisely as possible the number of those killed both before and during the massacre, as well as the number who were taken as prisoners to Canada. No doubt the figure of about 185 killed, as given in the book *Betrayals* by Ian Steele, is well reasoned and supported by documentary evidence, even though the deaths of undocumented camp followers might raise this figure somewhat. However, it is important that what happened following the surrender at Fort William Henry not be allowed to slowly evolve into acceptable behavior. The "need" of Native warriors who had joined Montcalm's army to obtain booty cannot in some sense make them less accountable for their own behavior. The actual perpetrators of the massacre should not be forgotten nor their actions condoned.

The 1950s Dig and the Reconstruction

The 1950s excavations inside the ruins of Fort William Henry (fig. 8.1) revealed a tremendous amount of information about the final days at the fort, in the form of exploded mortar shells, cannonballs, skeletons, charred timbers and even the famous human scalp that had somehow survived the fires of 1757 but could not survive the more recent fire in 1967. Archeology helped to locate the foundations of many of the origi-

FIG. 8.1. Bastion of Fort William Henry before the excavation began in 1952. Courtesy of the Lake George Historical Association.

nal buildings, making the reconstruction of the barracks and bastions much more accurate; when combined with historical sources, the work by Stanley Gifford and his crew becomes eerily "real" for modern audiences. The artifacts are helping to tell the fort's story to thousands of visitors each summer, and the educational benefits have been enormous.

It is also important to remember that the purpose of this reconstructed fort (figs. 8.2 and 8.3) is to entertain. For many, the most enjoyable aspect of visiting the fort is to be photographed in the stocks or in the "irons" on the whipping post. Most visitors take the standard tour with a uniformed interpreter and watch the musket and cannon demonstrations, but they walk past the exhibit cases fairly quickly; they spend relatively little time peering into the displays or learning the historical particulars. That is unfortunate because Fort William Henry has some great stories to tell.

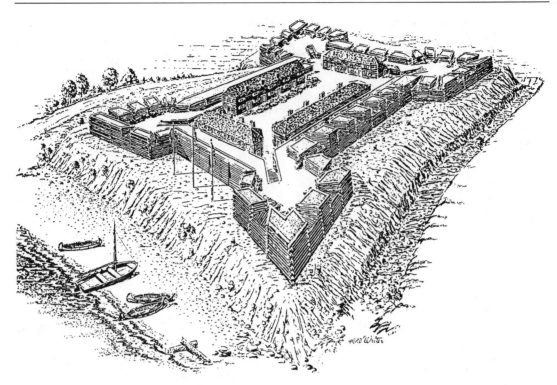

FIG. 8.2. The proposed reconstruction of Fort William Henry; the actual reconstruction did not include two of the barracks buildings shown here. Fort William Henry Museum.

The 1990s Archeological Dig

Perhaps the greatest benefit in conducting four more years of archeological research at Fort William Henry is that we were able to help visitors to better visualize life at a military outpost in the 1750s. Many had never seen eighteenth-century artifacts before, and for most it was fascinating to watch the dirty, broken fragments come out of the bottoms of our trenches and to then see them transported to our field laboratory for processing and interpretation. Many had never had a reason to take the French and Indian War very seriously before; yet as they stood alongside our trenches, they were watching archeologists systematically recording the "things" of the past, and they noticed how determined our students and volunteers were to tell a more accurate story with objects and building debris than James Fenimore Cooper ever could.

Finding ourselves on display wasn't always easy. Certainly, our most challenging experience came on July 4, 1997, when for the entire day our workers in the laboratory and our diggers in the trenches were surrounded by four thousand tourists, all shouting questions at us nonstop.

It is easy to write about the benefits of public education, but it's quite another thing to live through it!

We made several significant finds between 1997 and 2000, but these were not the sensational, media-grabbing discoveries that some might have hoped for. There were no bodies in the bottom of a barracks cellar, no tomahawk dangling from a grisly human skull, no cannons, swords, or muskets. The most exciting discovery for me personally was to descend to the bottom of the fort's well and learn how it had been constructed with a barrel lining (and to make it out alive!). For others, it may have been to find the main dump for the fort (Site 5), with its thousands of butchered animal bones that will soon tell us exactly what the soldiers were eating. And it was definitely significant when we discovered that the West Barracks had been reconstructed in the 1950s roughly fifteen feet west of its original foundation. This provided us with the unexpected opportunity to open up a major portion of one of the largest buildings inside the fort and to discover pins, wineglasses, and fine white, salt-glazed stoneware, evidence of the ordinary things that soldiers and

FIG. 8.3. The southwest bastion of Fort William Henry as it appears today. Lake George is in the background on the left.

officers used on a daily basis. And everywhere we dug there was evidence for burning. Charcoal and burned logs were to be found in almost every pit, reminding us of the holocaust that had consumed the fort at the very end.

Our excavations are over for now, but it has been rewarding to work amid the ruins of Fort William Henry, following in the footsteps of Colonel Monro, the Marquis de Montcalm, Père Pierre Roubaud, George Washington, James Fenimore Cooper, Harold Veeder, and others. The sad story of Fort William Henry will live on, only now we are able to feel a little bit closer to its final occupants, having toiled in the sands of what was once their home.

Tourists Say the Darndest Things!

One of the most entertaining aspects of working at a re-created fort is listening to the comments made by visitors, many of whom have never before viewed an archeological dig. Some of the comments overheard by my fellow diggers have been predictable, such as "Looking for gold?" or "Are you looking for anything in particular?" And many of our younger visitors have asked how to become an archeologist. Perhaps half of the tourists who visit Fort William Henry want to know whether we are looking for human remains, actually becoming irritated that we aren't. Some have told us that the only reason they visited the fort was to see bodies!

But sometimes visitors' comments have been more creative, occasionally verging on the bizarre. One of my favorites came from an elderly visitor who, after intently watching our diggers at work, commented to her friend, "They are so careful, you would almost think they are 'real' archeologists!" She had, of course, equated our group with the military reenactors who may often be found circulating throughout the fort.

Some of the other comments we have heard include the following:

"Are there any real archeologists here, or are they just high school students?"

"Showing bodies is part of history."

"Have you ever found anything?"

"I waited my whole life to see this!" (spoken by an eight year old to a six year old).

"Did you find any dinosaur bones yet?"

"What do you mean by 'prehistoric'? Does that mean before the dinosaurs?"

"If you find any gold, it's mine!"

"Did you find any war bodies yet?"

"With all the rocks [in the sifting screen], how can you tell which are the arrowheads?"

"Mommy, have they dug to the Devil yet?" (A little girl asked this of her mother.)

"Are you putting in land mines?" (asked while we were digging in the moat).

"I didn't know plastic could survive in the ground that long!" (spoken by a woman who noticed the black plastic we had used to line one of our pits).

"I saw your missing arrowhead in there!"

"I guess that's what you'll do to me if I'm not good!" (spoken by a visitor who noticed how hard our students were working in the hot sun).

"I'll bet they smell!" (One elderly tourist said this about us when he thought we couldn't hear him.)

"So which one of you is Indiana Jones?"

"This is where the diggers go to rest." (An attractive young woman said this to her child as she pointed at our laboratory, where all of the artifacts were being processed.)

"I lost a Spanish doubloon out here—have you found it yet?"

"Do you find it frustrating when you don't find anything?"

"Do you have a bucket?" (asked of a digger who was quite obviously carrying a bucket).

"Yes, son, they're looking for treasure." (A father said this to his young son.)

"Yes, son, they're looking for dead Indians." (Another father said this to *his* son.)

"Are they looking for Civil War stuff?" (A tourist was overheard saying this after he had already been inside the fort for an hour or more.)

"When are you going to get through those bones and down to the good stuff?" (spoken by one of the interpretive staff at the fort).

(Five-year-old twins): "How do they know where to dig? Where are the X's?"

(Their mother's response): "Oh, you mean X marks the spot of the buried treasure?"

(The twins): "Yes."

(Their mother): "They don't need X's."

"Were the Indians really a match for us since all they had were bows and arrows?"

"Are the artifacts that you find today going to be on sale in the gift shop?"

One woman visitor, when she saw the top of the fort's well, which is now covered with a metal grate, told her children, "This is where they cooked their food. This was their barbecue."

Summary of Artifacts Excavated at Fort William Henry

The following table is a site-by-site summary of some of the more meaningful categories of artifacts that were excavated at Fort William Henry between 1997 and 2000. They have been divided into those found on the inside as opposed to the outside of the reconstructed fort, and it is immediately apparent that at least 70–80 percent of all artifacts recovered were found either within the foundation of the West Barracks (Sites 4 and 8) or in the dump that lies just east of the fort (Site 5). No counts are included for sites 7, 10, and 11 because the numbers were very low.

Some significant artifact categories, such as nails and window glass, are not listed because of the difficulty in distinguishing between those from the 1750s and those from later periods.

Table 2.1
Artifacts Recovered from Fort William Henry, 1997–2000, inside the Reconstructed Fort

Artifacts	Site 3: Well	Site 2: Southeast corner of parade ground	Site 4: North end of parade ground	Site 6: South end of parade ground	Sites 4 and 8: Northwest corner of parade ground and West Barracks
Ceramic sherds					
Redware	2	3	14	3	119
Delft	1	1	10	87	82
Slip-decorated, buff-bodied earthenware	0	0	1	0	12
White salt-glazed stoneware	0	0	13	5	239
Gray salt-glazed stoneware	6	3	3	3	64
Brown salt-glazed stoneware	0	0	0	0	2
Unrefined stoneware	0	1	2	4	14
Porcelain	4	2	4	6	72

Table 2.1 cont.

Artifacts	Site 3: Well	Site 2: Southeast corner of parade ground	Site 4: North end of parade ground	Site 6: South end of parade ground	Sites 4 and 8: Northwest corner of parade ground and West Barracks
Glass					
Wine bottle fragments	136	3	71	58	199
Case bottle fragments	1	0	9	3	22
Tableware fragments	0	2	1	3	77
Vial fragments	0	0	48	6	30
Armaments					
Musket balls (complete)	12	6	41	4	103
Musket balls (flattened)	0	0	0	2	0
Musket balls with tooth marks	0	0	0	0	1
Musket ball fragments	0	1	2	1	3
Cut lead shot	9	0	5	0	0
Lead sprue	0	0	1	1	1
Lead slag (from casting balls)	0	18	310	0	68
Grapeshot	0	0	0	0	3
Canister shot	0	0	13	0	4
Mortar shell fragments	0	0	7	0	8
Worms	0	0	0	0	1
Worm fragments	0	0	1	0	0
Gunflints, British	0	0	8	3	16
Gunflint fragments, British	0	1	7	0	5
Gunflints, French	3	1	3	2	32
Gunflint fragments, French	0	1	6	0	5
Gunflints, burned	0	1	3	2	16
Bayonet fragments	0	0	0	0	2
Musket parts	0	0	0	0	1
Gun furniture	0	0	0	0	2
Scabbard hook with leather	0	0	1	0	0
Utilitarian					
Cast-iron pot/kettle fragments	0	0	1	0	1
Hinge fragment	0	0	0	0	1
Door handle	0	0	1	0	0
Felling ax	1	0	1	0	0
Fishhooks	0	0	0	1	2
Cutlery					
Knives	0	0	0	0	2
Forks	0	0	0	0	2
Spoons	0	1	1	0	1

Artifacts	Site 3: Well	Site 2: Southeast corner of parade ground	Site 4: North end of parade ground	Site 6: South end of parade ground	Sites 4 and 8: Northwest corner of parade ground and West Barracks
Sewing equipment					
Pins	0	0	2	1	18
Needles	0	0	0	0	1
Thimbles	0	0	0	0	1
Scissors	0	0	0	0	1
Personal adornments					
Buttons, metal	0	1	7	3	36
Buttons, wood	1	0	0	0	1
Buttons, bone	0	0	1	0	0
Buttons, regimental	0	0	1[a]	0	2[b]
Cuff links	0	0	0	2	3
Rings	0	0	0	0	1
Buckles	0	0	2	0	16
Coins					
British halfpennies	0	0	1 (1730)	0	3
Spanish silver reales	0	0	0	0	1
Animal bone and tooth fragments	187[c]	483	2,913	394	7,448

[a] Second Battalion Pennsylvania.

[b] First Battalion Pennsylvania; Twenty-second Regiment.

[c] This total does not include the 39 bones from a duck or goose skeleton.

Table 2.2
Artifacts Recovered from Fort William Henry, 1997–2000, outside the Reconstructed Fort

Artifacts	Site 1: Edge of Military Cemetery	Site 5: Dump East of Fort	Site 9: Moat	Site 13: Near Tower Theater
Ceramic Sherds				
Redware	36	70	10	4
Delft	39	138	1	0
Slip-decorated, buff-bodied earthenware	0	2	0	0
White salt-glazed stoneware	3	162	1	1
Gray salt-glazed stoneware	29	74	2	0
Unrefined stoneware	57	10	1	0

Table 2.2 cont.

Artifacts	Site 1: Edge of Military Cemetery	Site 5: Dump East of Fort	Site 9: Moat	Site 13: Near Tower Theater
Porcelain	219	57	2	0
Glass				
Wine bottle fragments	152	367	17	1
Case bottle fragments	0	177	0	0
Tableware fragments	85	105	6	0
Vial fragments	7	32	5	0
Armaments				
Musket balls (complete)	0	75	5	1
Musket balls (flattened)	0	1	0	0
Musket ball fragments	0	1	0	0
Lead sprue (split off from molds)	0	2	0	0
Lead slag (from casting balls)	7	55	3	0
Grapeshot	0	9	0	0
Grapeshot fragments	0	1	0	0
Canister shot	0	1	0	0
Mortar shell fragments	0	3	0	0
Worms	0	1	0	0
Gunflints, British	0	27	0	0
Gunflint fragments, British	1	8	0	0
Gunflints, French	1	19	0	0
Gunflint fragments, French	2	13	0	0
Gunflints, burned	0	9	0	0
Utilitarian				
Cast-iron pot/kettle fragments	0	1	0	0
Hinge fragment	0	1	0	0
Lock plate	0	1	0	0
Fishhooks	1	0	0	0
Cutlery				
Knives	1	3	0	0
Spoons	1	1	0	0
Sewing equipment				
Scissors	1	0	0	0
Pins	3	1	0	0
Personal adornments				
Buttons, metal	5	36	0	0
Buttons, wood	1	0	0	0
Cuff links	0	3	0	0
Buckles	1	5	0	0
Musical instruments				
Mouth harps (Jew's harps)	0	2	0	0

Artifacts	Site 1: Edge of Military Cemetery	Site 5: Dump East of Fort	Site 9: Moat	Site 13: Near Tower Theater
Coins				
British halfpennies	0	2	0	0
Spanish silver reales	0	1	0	0
Animal bone and tooth fragments	594	15,853[a]	0	75

[a] This total does not include the horn core from a cow or ox.

Further Reading

Anderson, Fred. *A People's Army: Massachusetts Soldiers and Society in the Seven Years' War*. Chapel Hill: University of North Carolina Press, 1984.

———. *Crucible of War: The Seven Years' War and the Fate of Empire in British North America, 1754–1766*. New York: Alfred A. Knopf, 2000.

Axtell, James, and William C. Sturtevant. "The Unkindest Cut, or Who Invented Scalping?" *William and Mary Quarterly*, 37, 3 (1980):451–72.

Baker, Brenda J., and Christina B. Rieth. "Beyond the Massacre: Historic and Prehistoric Activity at Fort William Henry." *Northeast Anthropology* 60 (2000):45–61.

Beckett, James A. "The Real 'Natty,' an Elder Brother: From *The Otsego Farmer*, July 19, 1912." *Proceedings of the New York State Historical Association* 17 (1917):187–92.

Bellico, Russell P. *Chronicles of Lake George: Journeys in War and Peace*. Fleischmanns, N.Y.: Purple Mountain Press, 1995.

Bellico, Russell P., Bob Benway, Tim Cordell, John Farrell, Scott Padeni, and Joseph W. Zarzynski. *Colonial Wars of Lake George Self-Guided Tour*. Bateaux Below, 1996.

Birdsall, Rev. Ralph. "Fenimore Cooper in Cooperstown." *Proceedings of the New York State Historical Association* 16 (1917):137–49.

Bougainville, Louis Antoine de. *Adventure in the Wilderness: The American Journals of Louis Antoine de Bougainville 1756–1760*. Translated and edited by Edward P. Hamilton. Norman: University of Oklahoma Press, 1964.

Brasser, T. J. "Mahican." In *Handbook of North American Indians*: Vol. 15. *Northeast*, pp. 198–212. Washington, D.C.: Smithsonian Institution, 1978.

Cooper, James Fenimore. *The Last of the Mohicans*. 1826; reprint New York: Penguin Books, 1980.

Cuneo, John R. *Robert Rogers of the Rangers*. Ticonderoga, N.Y.: Fort Ticonderoga Museum, 1988.

Dodge, Edward J. *Relief Is Greatly Wanted: The Battle of Fort William Henry*. Bowie, Md.: Heritage Books, 1998.

Dunn, Shirley W. *The Mohicans and Their Land, 1609–1730*. Fleischmanns, N.Y.: Purple Mountain Press, 1994.

Fitch, Jabez, Jr. *The Diary of Jabez Fitch, Jr. in the French and Indian War, 1757*. 2nd ed. Fort Edward, N.Y.: Rogers Island Historical Association, 1968. Publication no. 1.

Funk, Robert E. "Recent Contributions to Hudson Valley Prehistory." *New York State Museum Memoir*, no. 22. Albany: New York State Museum, 1976.

Gifford, Stanley M. *Fort Wm. Henry: A History*. Lake George, N.Y.: Fort William Henry, 1955.

Holden, James Austin. "The Last of the Mohicans, Cooper's Historical Inventions, and His Cave." *Proceedings of the New York State Historical Association* 16 (1917):212–55.

Kochan, James L., ed. "Joseph Frye's Journal and Map of the Siege of Fort William Henry, 1757." *Bulletin of the Fort Ticonderoga Museum* 15 (1993): 339–61.

Liston, Maria A., and Brenda J. Baker. "Military Burials at Fort William Henry." Pp. 11–16 in *Military Sites of the Hudson River, Lake George, and Lake Champlain Corridor*, ed. David R. Starbuck. Queensbury, NY: Adirondack Community College, 1994.

———. "Reconstructing the Massacre at Fort William Henry, New York." *International Journal of Osteoarchaeology* 6 (1995):28–41.

Lossing, Benson J. *The Pictorial Field-Book of the Revolution.* 2 vols. New York: Harper & Brothers, 1851.

Magee, James A. "A Brief Outline of the Military Events Which Took Place at Lake George during the Colonial and Revolutionary Period . . ." Manuscript on file, Fort William Henry, Lake George, N.Y., 1965.

Parker, Arthur C. "The Archeological History of New York." *New York State Museum Bulletin*, nos. 235, 236. Albany: University of the State of New York, 1920.

Parkman, Francis. *Montcalm and Wolfe.* New York: Collier Books, 1962.

Ritchie, William A. *The Archaeology of New York State.* Harrison, N.Y.: Harbor Hill Books, 1980.

Snow, Dean R. *The Archaeology of New England.* New York: Academic Press, 1980.

Starbuck, David R. "A Retrospective on Archaeology at Fort William Henry, 1952–1993: Retelling the Tale of *The Last of the Mohicans.*" *Northeast Historical Archaeology* 20 (1991):8–26.

———. "Anatomy of a Massacre." *Archaeology* 46 (November/December 1993): 42–46.

———. "The Big Dig: Looking for Traces of Fort William Henry's Brutal Past." *Adirondack Life* 29 (September/October 1998):44–49, 77–78.

———. *The Great Warpath.* Hanover, N.H.: University Press of New England, 1999.

———. "Beneath the Bubblegum." *Archaeology* 54 (January/February 2001): 22–23.

Steegmann, A. T., Jr., and P. A. Haseley. "Stature Variation in the British American Colonies: French and Indian War Records, 1755–1763." *American Journal of Physical Anthropology* 75 (1988):413–21.

Steele, Ian K. *Betrayals: Fort William Henry and the "Massacre."* New York: Oxford University Press, 1990.

Taylor, Alan. *William Cooper's Town.* New York: Alfred A. Knopf, 1995.

Todish, Timothy J. *America's First First World War: The French and Indian War. 1754–1763.* Ogden, Utah: Eagle's View Publishing Co., 1988.

———. "Triumph and Tragedy: The Siege of Fort William Henry," pt. 1. *Muzzleloader*, November/December 1992, pp. 36–40.

———. "Triumph and Tragedy: The Siege of Fort William Henry," pt. 2. *Muzzleloader*, January/February 1993, pp. 31–36.

Twain, Mark. "Fenimore Cooper's Literary Offenses." In *The Complete Humorous Sketches and Tales of Mark Twain*, ed. Charles Neider, pp. 631–42. 1895; reprinted New York: Doubleday, 1961.

Woods, Lynn. "A History in Fragments." *Adirondack Life* 25, 7 (1994):30–37, 61, 68–71, 78–79.

Index